Powerful Encounters in the GOD Realm

POWERFUL ENCOUNTERS
in the GOD REALM

Testimonies and Teachings
of Today's Frontline Generals

Unless otherwise noted, Scriptures are taken from the NEW AMERICAN STANDARD BIBLE®, Copyright © 1960,1962,1963,1968,1971,1972,1973,1975,1977,1995 by The Lockman Foundation. Used by permission.

Scripture quotations marked "ESV" are from the ESV Bible® (The Holy Bible, English Standard Version®), copyright © 2001 by Crossway Bibles, a publishing ministry of Good News Publishers. Used by permission. All rights reserved.

Scripture quotatios marked NIV are from THE HOLY BIBLE, NEW INTERNATIONAL VERSION®, NIV® Copyright © 1973, 1978, 1984, 2011 by Biblica, Inc.™ Used by permission. All rights reserved worldwide.

Scripture quotations marked "AMP" are taken from the Amplified® Bible, Copyright © 1954, 1958, 1962, 1964, 1965, 1987 by The Lockman Foundation. Used by permission.

Scripture quotations marked "MSG" are taken from The Message. Copyright 1993, 1994, 1995, 1996, 2000, 2001, 2002. Used by permission of NavPress Publishing Group.

Scripture quotations marked "NKJV" are taken from the New King James Version. Copyright © 1982 by Thomas Nelson, Inc. Used by permission. All rights reserved.

Published by XP Publishing
A department of Christian Services Association
P.O. Box 1017, Maricopa, Arizona 85139
www.XPpublishing.com

ISBN: 978-1-936101-60-3

XPpublishing.com

Printed in the United States of America
For Worldwide Distribution

Dedicated to those who are hungry

for more of HIM!

CONTENTS

From Patricia King 9

1. The Realm of Mercy – Patricia King 11

2. Be with Him Where He is – Faytene Grasseschi 25

3. Manna and Jewels from the Glory Realm – Kaye Beyer 41

4. An Evening Without God – Darren Wilson 51

5. Jesus Encounters in the Supernatural – Stacey Campbell 67

6. Healings and Miracles in the Glory – Joan Hunter 83

7. Branded by the Fire of Love – Georgian Banov 95

8. Encountering the Heavenly Realm – Patricia King 113

9. God of the Burning Heart – Julie Meyer 123

10. It's Your Season for Angelic Encounters – Randy DeMain 137

11. Discerning Angels and Demons – Matt Sorger 151

12. Healing in the Glory Realm – Katie Souza 169

13. In the Presence of Angels – Joshua Mills 185

14. Day of the Prophetic Warrior – Jerame Nelson 201

15. Running with God – Samuel Robinson 213

Authors and Resources – 227

From Patricia King

My desire for everyone who reads this devotional is that you grow in personal encounters with God. To live in the God-realm is to know Him. Like Moses, may you enter the presence of His glory and encounter Him face-to-face as one meets with a friend. He is longing to touch you and draw you into the deepest places of His heart. May you experience His presence ... His rest ... His goodness ... His glorious name! May you enjoy all the days of your life, "Powerful Encounters in the God-Realm."

> Now Moses used to take the tent and pitch it outside the camp, a good distance from the camp, and he called it the tent of meeting...
>
> Whenever Moses entered the tent, the pillar of cloud would descend and stand at the entrance of the tent, and the Lord would speak with Moses.
>
> Thus the Lord used to speak to Moses face to face, just as a man speaks to his friend.
>
> ...Now therefore I pray You, if I have found favor in Your sight, let me know Your ways that I may know You, so that I may find favor in Your sight...

And He said, "My presence shall go with you, and I will give you rest."

Then Moses said, "I pray You, show me Your glory!"

And He said, "I myself will make all My goodness pass before you, and will proclaim the name of the Lord before you..."

Exodus 33:7,9,11,13,14,18,19

THE REALM OF MERCY

PATRICIA KING

CHAPTER ONE

Before I came to Christ, I was a mess: addicted to alcohol, emotionally out of control, mentally confused, and ready for a psychiatric hospital. I felt worthless and dark all the way to the core of my being. Few realized the predicament I was in because I could function in day-to-day tasks and pull myself together when needed. However, I was in constant torment – fighting guilt, condemnation, shame, and hopelessness. I was enslaved by lies, deception, and depression.

I searched in many ways for relief and understanding of my problems. I took night school college courses in psychology and human behavior, hoping to discover insights for my deliverance. I read self-help books, attended health and well-being seminars. I did yoga, engaged in new age practices, tried mantras, meditation, and controlled-breathing techniques that promised peace of mind.

I did everything I could think of, but nothing helped. In fact, the more I tried the more out of control I became. My outbursts of anger and rage put at risk my two little children whom I loved with all my heart. I attempted to drown my guilt with alcohol and indulged during the day, sometimes passing out, even when the children were awake. I felt completely alone, beyond help or hope, and afraid to share my problems with anyone. How could I reveal what was going on behind closed doors, and who could I tell? Fear of exposure plagued me. Fear of rejection beleaguered me.

In addition, I was experiencing unpredictable epileptic seizures, so I was also exploring medical solutions. After brain scans, EEGs and other diagnostic tests, the doctors were bewildered. Their tests showed no abnormalities and yet I continued to suffer convulsions and blackouts on a regular basis.

After exhausting all my options, I concluded there was no hope for me. My children were in danger and I needed to do whatever it took to make sure they were safe. So, I made the decision to admit to my rages and commit myself to psychiatric care. My greatest fear was that my children would be taken away from me and that once committed to a psych ward, I would never be released. Looking back, I can see this was irrational, but at the time this apprehension seemed very real. My disturbed and troubled mind was exhausted and I saw everything through a distorted perception. I felt evil to the core and hated the things I said and did. No one had to tell me that I was a sinner; I knew I was, but did not know how to change. All my efforts to overcome my problems had failed, and I despised myself.

Finally, I mustered the courage to create a concrete plan of action. I was ready to bring everything into the light, but first I wanted to make sure that both my sons were christened. This was a tradition in our family, although I did not really understand what it meant. My warped reasoning was that if I never came out of the psych hospital, I would possibly see the boys in heaven, providing they had been ceremonially christened in the Anglican church.

The phone book gave me the number for the local Anglican church, and when I called the pastor himself answered. I explained that I was in a crisis and needed his "christening services" the next Sunday. He was silent for a moment, cleared his throat, and then proceeded to outline the pre-qualifications for the ceremony, which included a series of eight mandatory classes for the parents. I panicked because I felt that my need was urgent, but right then I did not feel safe divulging my "secret." Rage began to build in me. However, before I let him have it with a stream of vile profanities, I slammed the phone down, terminating the call. I was furious. "How dare that man deny me this service," I repeated over and over as I paced up and down the hallway of our home trying to let off steam. Within thirty minutes, my doorbell rang. Quickly composing myself, I answered the door only to find the pastor I had been railing against standing on my front porch with a big smile. "Are you Patricia?" he asked. He introduced himself, explaining that when I hung up he looked me up in the phone book and found my address. Needless to say, I was not happy to see him.

He made his way into my kitchen, sat down at the table and proceeded to open the conversation with questions about my life. I faked a smile and attempted to impress him. I knew he was a spiritual man so I endeavored to share some of the profound spiritual disciplines I had learned from the New Age movement. "Surely that would astound him and convince him of my spirituality," I thought. He listened intently, while his face hid shock and disagreement. After listening to me rave about my spirituality for a while, he shared about his personal encounter with God. He told me that he had been an Anglican priest for seventeen years but had only known God in a *personal* way for the last two years. He further explained that it is possible to know about God, engage in Christian traditions, and even "talk the talk," yet not know God personally.

He had gone through the motions of the liturgy, studied in seminary, yet never knew God in a personal and meaningful way. He had held to mere forms of godliness for 15 years prior to coming to Christ. He shared with me about being "born-again" and how the Lord could give me a *brand new life*. He explained that the Lord would wash all the sin, guilt, and shame of the past away and make all things new. This was "good news" to me, but I found it difficult to believe that God could accept me as I was – after all, He is perfect and how could I ever face Him? The pastor invited me to attend a prayer group meeting just up the street.

Several nights later, when I arrived at the prayer meeting, I was overwhelmed with the love and peace I felt as I entered the home. After the pastor's visit, he requested they pray for me. I, however, was not aware that they had been praying for days against the enemy's grip on my life and were claiming the promises of God for my salvation. That evening, they sang songs, prayed aloud, and shared testimonies of how Jesus forgave them of all their sin and gave them a new beginning. One after another, I heard the wonderful stories of how Christ had transformed their lives. Oh, how I wanted the freedom they had, but I still wondered if God could forgive the likes of me and give me a brand new life, too. I so desired Him, but I was unsure He wanted me.

After the meeting, I returned home and knelt on my living room floor. It was around midnight when I cried out to God. With simple, desperate words from my heart, I said, "Jesus, I am such a mess and I feel so evil inside. Those people at the meeting said that

You forgave their sins and gave them a brand new life. I have nothing good to offer You, but I was wondering, would you come into *my* heart anyway and forgive *my* sin?"

I honestly did not know if Jesus would forgive me or not. I was hoping He would but was unsure that He would want to. To my delight, He did not hesitate for a moment. I actually felt Him enter my life; I can only describe the feeling as being filled with liquid love. I experienced a tangible sensation of the weight of my guilt, shame, and sin leaving me. His life-giving love filled me to the core of my being that night. It was a love I didn't deserve, but He was not concerned about what I did or did not deserve – this was a gift. This was mercy. I felt brand new and clean inside. His presence was so amazing! He captured my heart with the very essence of love and I knew that He would be with me forever. I would love Him and serve Him all the days of my life. He knew every detail of my "secrets" yet He loved me perfectly. One definition of mercy is, "not getting what you deserve." I deserved judgment, condemnation, punishment, rejection, and eternal damnation, but instead I received forgiveness, cleansing, love, kindness, friendship, and a brand new life. Oh yes, *that* is MERCY.

I will never forget that night, the moment I entered the realm of Christ's mercy and grace and was granted eternal life. Jesus and I are entwined together for eternity because of mercy. How I love that realm. Oh, where would I be without His glorious mercy?

Where would you be?

Jesus and I are entwined together for eternity because of mercy.
Oh, where would I be without His glorious mercy?
Where would you be?

THE DIVINE EXCHANGE

A number of years later, I hurt a close friend very deeply. I did not intend to, but I made a foolish choice without considering the consequence. When I realized what I had done, I asked my friend to forgive me. I was very broken and truly repentant. They refused to grant forgiveness and I was devastated; I began beating myself up emotionally with self-condemnation. For several years, every time I thought of that situation I would inflict myself again. I'd think, "How could I have been so insensitive? Why wasn't I smart enough to see it as it was? How could I have said that? How could I have done it?" I could not forgive myself and once again lived in a prison of condemnation, guilt, and shame.

One day when I was in the midst of a "beat-myself-up session," the Lord spoke to me and said, "You did not do that!" I argued with Him and rehearsed the situation again with every detail to prove that it was only fitting that I take the blame. He repeated, "You did not do that!" I filled in more details of the situation, just in case He had forgotten, but once again, He said, "You did not do that!" When I was ready to point out more reasons for my guilt, He stated emphatically, "I DID IT!" I was shocked to hear what was obviously absurd, so I responded, "No, Jesus, I did it. You are perfect. There is no way You did that."

Then Jesus responded, "Two thousand years ago, I took full responsibility for this sin. I became this sin and set you free. In exchange, I gave you My righteousness. This is no longer your issue; it is Mine. I also paid the full penalty for this violation. It became My responsibility, not yours. And if your friend has a grievance, they need to come to Me, because it is *Mine*, not yours."

I burst into tears. I did not deserve this act of love … no one does. He is so beautiful and merciful! He gently explained later that day, as I was struggling to let go of my guilt, that every time I chose to take the weight of responsibility upon myself for a sin I had asked Him to forgive, I was denying Him and the work He completed at Calvary.

He taught me that when I beat myself up, I was choosing to be a victim rather than the victor He had recreated me to be in Him. He revealed that I was operating in a religious spirit. A judgmental religious spirit always wars against mercy and discounts the meaning of the Cross by demanding that you pay in some way for your sins and mistakes. Mercy, however, triumphs over judgment.

A judgmental religious spirit always wars against mercy and discounts the meaning of the Cross by demanding that you pay in some way for your sins and mistakes. Mercy, however, triumphs over judgment.

Once again, the mercy of Christ opened my prison door and set me free. The fear of the Lord enabled me to forgive myself and repent from self-inflicting punishment, guilt, and shame. Mercy cleansed me … mercy released me.

I met a woman a while back, who had committed adultery. She encountered a man at her workplace that she was attracted to; over a number of months they connected emotionally. After work, they started meeting occasionally for dinner or a movie. They spent a great deal of time calling and texting each other, and they would lie to their spouses to cover up what was really going on in their growing emotional attachment. The relationship finally became sexual. Her husband discovered the affair by accidentally reading an email she had written her lover. When he confronted her, she admitted that she was in love with another man. Her husband was furious and devastated. In his pain, he left the home; she became despondent and ended the illicit relationship!

As the songwriter says,
"We owed a debt we could not pay;
He paid a debt He did not owe."
THIS IS THE MERCY REALM!

Daily, she brutally condemned herself, hating what she had done, and she became deeply depressed. After a year, her husband returned and told her that he still loved her, wanted to forgive her and start all over. Deeply touched by his forgiveness, they started afresh. However, she could not forgive herself. Over and over again, she would tell her husband how terrible she felt about what she had done. He tried to assure her that she was forgiven but she would not let go of her offense. No matter what he said to comfort her, she could not forgive herself.

She was prisoner to a religious spirit. No one can pay the price for his or her own sin. It is impossible! If we do not receive God's mercy, nothing can dissolve our guilt ... nothing! Pride is ruling us if we even think for a moment that we could accomplish such a task. Only the mercy of Christ ... only His mercy can give us relief from our guilt! As the songwriter says, "We owed a debt we could not pay; He paid a debt He did not owe." THIS IS THE MERCY REALM!

Finally, the woman entered counseling and became convicted of her religious attempts to pay for her past sin. She was awakened to behold the mercy of God. What a day of deliverance that was for her. She decided to make the devil sorry he ever tried to destroy their marriage by making up for the time they had lost together and by rebuilding their marriage into something better than before. She and her husband invested much time and focus into their relationship. The Lord blessed their faith and persistence; even though it was not always easy, they were determined. Their children also began to heal and the entire family experienced a season of new beginnings. Mercy had given them a brand new start. Mercy had opened the door to healing and restoration.

THE MERCY SEAT

In the book of Exodus, Chapter 25, we find God speaking to Moses regarding the building of the tabernacle in the wilderness. In verse 40, God told Moses to build "according to the pattern." The pattern included the construction of the inner court, which often symbolizes the inner man. God instructed Moses to build the Ark of the Covenant before anything else. The Ark represents the finished work of the Cross. He told Moses to build the mercy seat on top of the Ark. The golden wings of the cherubim were to spread over the mercy seat; this was where God's Shekinah glory dwelt and where God spoke to Moses concerning Israel. God did not speak from the *judgment seat* but from the *mercy seat*. This seat of mercy was established on the covenant Christ created through His finished work on the Cross. What a glorious gospel!

The mercy seat was located in the midst of the inner court. The tabernacle wasn't built from the outside in but from the inside out. We do not become established in Christ by getting our "outer" behavior aligned but by allowing the "inner" work of the Cross to touch us with His mercy. Jesus said, "From [your] innermost being will flow rivers of living water" (John 7:38).

The holy gift of eternal life given to us through His amazing mercy is ours, and it has forever released us from the guilt and punishment we deserve – mercy always triumphs over judgment.

The Impact of Mercy

I have discovered that when I experience the mercy realm, I am powerfully motivated from the heart to surrender more of my life to Him. Self-effort and attempts to apply the law to fix myself, however, have the opposite effect. In fact, the harder I try, the more I seem to fail. Self-effort and striving to fulfill the law actually makes me captive to hopelessness, failure, futile striving, and self-condemnation. Once again, I find myself a failure, and the cycle of self-focus and religious bondage is re-established. However, when I focus on the mercy of God and soak in the freedom of His unconditional love, I am naturally motivated to live for Him; His righteous life flows from inside out to change the way I interact with my world and the people in it.

The holy gift of eternal life given to us through His amazing mercy is ours, and it has forever released us from the guilt and punishment we deserve – mercy always triumphs over judgment.

God's mercy should never be taken lightly or taken for granted. It hurts me when I see people deliberately violate the law of God and say things like, "Well, praise God for His mercy." They have no remorse or repentance. They are abusing His goodness and grace. His mercy is very holy and should be treated as sacred. It is a healing balm for the sin-sick soul, not a license for sinful behavior.

It should be received with deep reverence and respect. The mercy realm is a holy realm.

Freely you have received, freely give.

Everyone faces difficulties in life. It is part of the journey through our earthly existence. There will be those who hurt you deeply and those who you witness hurting others. It is easy and "natural" to judge a person for the wrong they do, but it takes the God-nature arising from our inner man to show them mercy.

I need mercy every day; therefore, I cannot afford to withhold mercy from others. In the Kingdom of God, the measure that we give to others will be given to us in return – pressed down, shaken together, and running over (see Luke 6:37-38). I want to live all my days established on the mercy seat. I have freely received His mercy in abundance, so it is my pleasure to sow it into the lives of others.

Have you had a powerful encounter with His mercy? If not, soak or meditate on His mercy right now. He loves you so deeply that two thousand years ago, He took responsibility for your sin. He actually *became your sin* and gave you His righteousness in exchange for it.

You can have a fresh start in life *today* by receiving His mercy ... and living to sow mercy into the lives of others. What a way to live! Will you enter the glorious realm of His grace and mercy and find your mercy seat?

BE WITH HIM WHERE HE IS AND SEE THE GLORY OF HIS LIBERATING LOVE

FAYTENE GRASSESCHI

CHAPTER TWO

Father, I desire that they also, whom You have given
Me, *be with Me* where I am, *so that they may see My
glory* which You have given Me.

(John 17:24 emphasis added)

I love how the most impacting encounters with God often happen when you least expect them. In an instant, God can invade the *normal* with His "non-normalness." In what feels like the blink of an eye, you can find your world "rocked."

ONE OF THOSE TIMES

It happened one night during a very sweet time of worship. The kind of worship I love: dim lights, just you and Holy Spirit, a few simple chords on the piano, and your spirit totally locked on the Divine One. It was a sweet time of singing songs of love and exaltation to Jesus. I was loving every moment. I do not remember exactly what I was singing but it was something like, "God, You are awesome, I love You, You have always been so kind, holy, holy, holy…" Though I do not remember the words, I do remember that it was wonderful. God's presence was tangible. My heart was being filled with Him as I sang love songs before His throne.

It was so sweet being focused solely on Him – no agenda, no ministry assignment to pray for, or requests, or discernment questions. It was such a sweet time of simple worship – until I detected a strange sense of detachment on His part. The best way I can describe it: it was like being in a conversation with someone you are close to and, as you share something with them, you sense their mind in another place. It isn't that they do not love you or care deeply about what you are sharing. They do, but something is bothering them. They are distracted and you sense it. Their mind is in another place. That was what I was picking up from the Lord. He loved me and my worship, but His heart was heavy with a distraction. Something was bugging Him and as my heart became more sensitive to His through worship, I could feel His preoccupation.

Because I love Him and desire to be connected with Him, at that point my focus shifted away from my song to wondering where His mind was. As I continued to play lightly on the keys, I turned my heart toward His and queried, "What is it, Lord? What is on Your heart? What is on Your mind? What is distracting You?"

IN AN INSTANT, I WAS TAKEN INTO A VISION

I do not know about you, but I sometimes struggle to find words that are adequate to describe things I see, feel, or experience in the spirit realm, especially when it rocks me to the core and is beyond human expression. This was one of those times, but I will do my best to describe it to you.

In my spirit, I was instantly taken to a dry and parched desert landscape that went as far as the eye could see. The soil all around was hard, cracked, lifeless, and hot, but the atmosphere was cold and uninviting. There was nothing comfortable about this place. Directly ahead in the far distance, I saw a range of huge, daunting mountains that also looked cold and harsh. They seemed to be at least a half-day's walk away, or more.

It was as if someone flung open the door to another realm and flooded my senses with the sights, sounds, and emotional distress of millions of terrified, hurting people.

The only thing I found comforting about this situation was the man standing about 50 yards in front of me; it was the man I love, Jesus. His back was to me (though I could see His right side a little) and he was staring straight ahead, fixated on the view of the mountains. The wind was blowing and His hair and garments flapped gently in the breeze. However, He did not seem to notice the wind; His gaze was locked intently ahead, and He had a very serious expression on His face. He was seemingly undistracted by my presence just yards behind Him. I could sense there was a force pulling Him in the direction He was staring. Nothing—not my presence, the wind, or the coldness of the landscape—was able to compete with whatever it was that attracted His attention. Observing this, a deep desire rose up in me to understand what it was He was seeing and feeling.

I asked Him, "What are You looking at? What is it?"

Specifically, I heard the sound of children, women, and the elderly whimpering in the night with hunger pains. I heard the weeping and muffled screams of little girls and boys imprisoned in dark and terrifying rooms and forced to have sex with diseased and demon-infested customers day and night. I heard the silent wail of babies being doused with acid and ripped apart limb by limb in their own mother's wombs and then the ringing of cash registers. I heard the sound of men and women in violent out-of-control arguments, the sound of fist upon flesh, whimpering, sobbing, and tears. I heard all these things at the same time. That was not it, however. Not only were these sounds rushing through my mind but I could feel the pain attached – I felt it all. It was horrific, terror upon terror, horror upon horror, nightmare upon nightmare, despair upon despair.

God was allowing me to drink of the "horror of the nations."

God was allowing me to drink of the "horror of the nations." The sound and the intensity of emotion that accompanied these unspeakable acts were unbearable. What a stark contrast to my nice cozy, comfortable worship song just a few moments prior.

What struck me even more forcibly about this visionary experience was the grief in God's loving heart for the pain suffered by so many of His creation. His heart was deeply distressed. He was intensely concerned because He is love, and love is always troubled and filled with compassion when the object of its affection is being hurt. The Lord was much more than "distracted" as I had originally thought. He was deeply grieved. This grief was propelling Him toward a mission that would end the suffering of these ones He loved so intensely.

What was more incredible was that – even though there was an overwhelming intensity with the entire scenario – in the midst of it all, He conveyed a quality of victory. He was determined to stop the torment, even if it had to be done one situation at a time. He was going into the conflict to rescue needy people. To fulfill His mandate to, "Vindicate the weak and fatherless; Do justice to the afflicted and destitute. Rescue the weak and needy; Deliver them out of the hand of the wicked" (Psalm 82:3-4).

I knew His heart was determined to move toward this mountain range of terror to fight for their deliverance and I wanted to go with Him. Because of love, everything in me desired to be with Him in that battle, no matter how intense and uncomfortable it might be. I wanted to be with Him where He was, so I purposed in my heart that I would not let Him go into that fight alone.

In the vision I rose up, stepped beside Him, put my hand in His, squeezed it, and said, "Jesus, I want to be with You where You are. If this is where You are – no matter how hard it is, no matter how uncomfortable, no matter how uninviting, no matter how painful it is – I want to be with You where You are." What a privilege! I thought. The moment my hand slipped into the warmth of His – the vision abruptly ended.

I said, "Jesus, I want to be with You where You are. If this is where You are – no matter how hard it is, no matter how uncomfortable, no matter how uninviting, no matter how painful it is – I want to be with You where You are."

Deeply impacted by what I had just experienced, I sat at the piano, stunned but still playing my simple chord progression, allowing the chilling and intimate reality of what had just happened to sink deeply into me. It settled upon me like a thick blanket and I was undone. No wonder He was distracted. The "horror of the nations" is absolutely piercing when we have "ears to hear" it. It was both an honor and agony to perceive it, and Jesus *always* hears the cries of those in anguish. "For the Lord hears the needy" (Psalm 69:33).

There are moments in life that mark you… that invade your heart with the heart of the Divine… that remind you of the "point." They are times that put a resolve in your soul and give you an impartation of strength to run forward in a way you never could prior to that encounter. There are events that empower and give you the juice to drive full-speed ahead. For me, this was one of those occasions. It was simple but powerful, deeply motivating, yet intensely intimate.

Be with Me Where I Am

I believe one of the most intimate prayers in all the Bible is found in John 17:24 when Jesus prayed, "Father, I desire that they also whom You gave Me may be with Me where I am" (NKJV). I find these words so telling, so powerful, so compassionate, so deep, and so romantic. When I meditate on them, I believe there are probably many reasons why Jesus would desire we be with Him where He is.

As Jesus prayed those words, He understood all things about eternity. He comprehended the reality of Heaven and the heights of ecstasy and glory to be experienced in His heavenly dominion. He also knew the torment, darkness, terror, and pure evil of hell.

Because He understood it all, and because He loves the world, I believe that He yearned for all humanity to be spared from the horror of hell. To be with Him where He was, in Heaven, would mean they would indeed be spared. This delighted Jesus' heart – and more than delighted – it drove Him. The desire what we would be with Him where He was in His eternal domain of Heaven is what drove Him to the Cross. That is extremely powerful. That is love.

Furthermore, He was perfectly united in love and spirit with the Father. Because of that unity, He would have felt the deep yearning of the Father to be reunited with mankind. Sin separated mankind from the Father and this broke the Father's heart. Jesus knew that. The reason Jesus knew that is because Jesus and the Father are perfectly united. Jesus longed for us to be with Him where He was, because this would mean that we would be reunited with the Father as well. To be with Jesus, and therefore with the Father, would have satisfied the Father's longing. What an incredible Son, Jesus is; He was consumed by the Father's desire for you and me.

The thing that touches me about the prayer in John 17:24 is that Christ also desired that we be with Him simply because He loves us and wants to be near us. That may be a simple revelation but it is a potent one. The uncomplicated reality of love is this: a person desires to be in the presence of the one they love. You make time in your day to connect with them in their world, you engage them conversationally, and you find ways to be present in their lives, even silently.

The thing that touches me about the prayer in John 17:24 is that Christ also desired that we be with Him simply because He loves us and wants to be near us. That may be a simple revelation but it is a potent one.

BEHOLDING HIS GLORY

In John 17:24, Jesus goes on, "I desire that they also whom You gave Me may be with Me where I am, *that they may behold My glory which You have given Me*" (emphasis added). Recently, I felt motivated to dig into this Scripture more deeply and I made a beautiful discovery.

The word "with" in this Scripture is the Greek word *metav*, which means, "to literally accompany someone or follow close behind them." Jesus' desire is that we would be with Him, following close behind Him, chasing after Him as He chases the dream of the Father to overthrow sin and its effect on the earth. This is so awesome! Jesus was saying and praying, "Father, I desire that they would be with Me, follow closely behind Me, radically pursuing Me where I am going." *Metav* does not give the sense of sitting on a couch and cuddling with Jesus – it implies motion. Jesus is going somewhere and it is His desire that we go with Him, following closely behind Him on His mission.

Moreover, the word "glory" is the Greek word *doxa*, commonly used in the New Testament and usually translated as glory, but it can also be rendered as "view, opinion, or judgment."

To behold His glory is not just seeing or experiencing His power and majesty, although that is part of it. It also means to behold His way of thinking – His mind, His viewpoint, His opinion, and His Word.

So, I believe Jesus was praying that we would be with Him, following closely behind Him while heeding His mind, view, and opinion. "Let this mind be in you which was also in Christ Jesus" (Philippians 2:5 NKJV).

To behold His glory is not just seeing or experiencing His power
and majesty, although that is part of it. It also means to behold
His way of thinking – His mind, His viewpoint, His opinion, and His
Word.

There are many reasons we can rush into battle to aid the oppressed, hungry, or afflicted. We should ask ourselves *why* we are doing what we do? What is the view, belief, or need that prompts us? Is it more about us or is it about the needy? Are we seeking to be the person of power for the hour? Are we looking for another self-promoting testimony, another notch in our belt, another story for the Sunday morning service, newsletter, or dinner table? Are we motivated by a sense of guilt, obligation, or religious duty to those watching us? What is *really* activating us?

Why do we do the things we do? Are we willing to "do good" simply for love? Are we willing to do works of compassion because He is doing them and we want to be like Him, doing the things we see the Father doing? Are we doing "good works" simply because He asked? Because we love Him and desire to do whatever He asks?

Jesus' motivations are always *pure*. His opinions are blemish free and that is why we can trust Him with childlike faith rather than become involved with skeptical questions or unbelief that slows down Kingdom momentum. We can trust His wisdom, His heart, His view – He sees things we do not always see. That is why we can follow Him into the darkness with complete trust even when we do not have a total understanding or when society is screaming a message opposite to His Word.

I believe Jesus' view always comes out of His love. He sees the pain and feels the anguish. He weeps with those who weep and, out of love, refuses to hold anything back in giving Himself for their liberty. He is the epitome of selfless motivation. His perspective is always motivated by the needs of others. It is never based on fear, self-preservation, or self-promotion – never on "self" anything. He stares at the mountain range of injustice with unwavering intent and envisions conquering it in fearless love.

For he will deliver the needy when he cries for help, the afflicted also, and him who has no helper (Psalm 72:12).

Running into the Darkness

Years ago, I began to pray radical prayers like, "Jesus, I want to go with You to the deepest and darkest places of the earth, the places few are willing to go. I want to run with You into the darkness so You don't have to go alone. If You are looking for a volunteer, here am I, Lord, send me." In 2000, that prayer took me to West Africa, specifically to the nation of Liberia.

Liberia was being ripped apart by civil war. I landed there during a window that lasted only a few months, between two massive outbreaks of national violence. While serving there in that short time of peace, I found children all around me without arms or legs, moms, dads, or peace of mind – all because of a senseless war. By the grace of God, every day I had the awesome privilege of being the hands and feet of Jesus to them, and I loved every moment of it. Most of all, I loved watching Jesus in action. Day after day I saw Him move heaven and earth to break into the lives of these children to save them.

On one such day, we saw Him supernaturally coordinate the schedules of over half-a-dozen adults. He put each of these adults in the right place at the right time – to enable us to rescue a few children at a village up the road from where I was staying. After a full day of hard work on their behalf and watching God perform miracle after miracle, I remember sitting on my bed that night filled with the intimate presence of Jesus. His presence was more tangible than I had ever felt up to that moment.

How can you not love a man who extended Himself so intently and effectively on the behalf of these hurting and frightened little ones? I fell even more in love with Him as I watched Him in action. If He had not helped us, those children would have died. The dance of deliverance we danced that day was deeply intimate – following His lead one step at a time. It was hard work, extremely unglamorous in the natural but as I watched Him in action, I felt more and more in love. It was so intimate. There is nothing like being with Him where He is and working alongside Him to fulfill His passion.

Ministering to His Heart, His Desire, His Pain

After a few months in Liberia, word spread about the work we were doing. Soon, every morning I awoke to a line of distressed people outside my door. Each one had a different story and a different need, but they all had one thing in common: they were desperate and needed help. I did not have an official missionary headquarters telling me what to do every day; it was just Jesus and me on the frontlines. I would simply open my door in the morning and start dealing with the situations as they stepped in front of me, one at a time. Every day I encountered God in His realm.

To know His mercy and goodness is to know His glory.

One night, after a full day of dealing with the needy, I sat praying in my missionary room at a Catholic nun's compound; they had graciously agreed to rent me a room. There was nothing but a sink, gray concrete walls, and a bed with a mosquito net over it to keep the night biters away. That evening, my prayer time took me back to Psalm 72, a Scripture dear to my heart.

Psalm 72 is an incredible Messianic Scripture that reveals God as King in His royal dominion. It speaks of an awesome King of justice and power. All the kings of the earth come and bow before Him. They bring Him gifts, defer to His awesomeness, and serve Him. It then goes on to say that He has concern for the needy, and the blood of the oppressed is precious in His sight. He will crush the head of the oppressor and His glory will spread throughout the earth. He uses His power to liberate and fight for the broken and destitute! How could you not love a man like this!

I then began to think about how God is all-knowing, all-seeing, and all-experiencing – omnipresent and omniscient – just like the vision, described earlier. He sees the "horror of the nations" continuously. He knows everything. He fully experiences it all, yet He has restrained Himself by allowing humanity to have free will.

God hates sin (Scripture is clear about that) because of how it hurts His created ones, and yet He does not force holiness on us. He beckons us by His Spirit to choose life and walk in His ways, but He does not twist our arm into submission; He grants us the power of choice. Tragically, many have not chosen "life" and that is why there is so much pain in the earth.

He gave the earth a solution. He overcame the power of evil through the work of the Cross and then extended His keys of authority to the Spirit-filled church. He left the job with us, "His body," we who are called to be the hands and feet of Jesus to a hurting, lost, and terrified world.

Matthew 25 says that whatever we have done to the hungry, the thirsty, the stranger, naked, sick, and those in prison, we have done to Him. When we feed the poor, visit the lonely, or clothe the naked, we literally do it to Him. Why? Because that is where He is – He is with them and when we are with them, we are with Him. "For He stands at the right hand of the needy" (Psalm 109:31.)

When we feed a hungry person, there is one less hungry person He suffers with – because He knows their pain and holds them in the arms of His heart. When we clothe the naked, He suffers from one less person's discomfort in this way. When we bring comfort to a lonely one, that's one less person whose loneliness He feels. To minister to their pain and their need is to minister to Him.

Mother Teresa said, "The miracle is not that we do the work, but that we are *happy* to do it." That is the heart of a true worshiper!

Mother Teresa expressed it well. When speaking of the poor she served, she said, "Each one of them is Jesus in disguise." And she also said, "The miracle is not that we do the work, but that we are *happy* to do it."

To serve Jesus in the poor was not drudgery but a joy for this woman. When you meditate on the magnitude of her task, the daily pressures she faced and the darkness that she so often encountered, you would wonder how she could say that this made her "happy."

Surely, there must have been another, more appropriate, word for her emotional state while standing in the midst of such need! No, "happy" was the perfect description. She loved Jesus and it was pure joy to be with Him where He was. To serve Jesus, regardless of where you find Him, is not a sacrifice but a joy if you are a lover.

The vision I shared at the beginning of this chapter remains with me to this day: I can still see Him standing in the midst of a desert, staring at a mountain range of horror and injustice. He is ready to break into the darkness and He desires that we come with Him.

I love encounters with God's glory that cause our jaws to drop with awe of the supernatural – I really do. I love encountering heaven. I love supernatural transportation, multiplication, healing, signs and wonders. I love and crave it all. However, more than anything, I am so thankful for God-encounters that bring us back to the basics of His humble heart, a heart that loved so deeply that it gave everything in brokenness and humility to end the "horror of the nations."

Let us hear the invitation of heaven beckoning us to enter into *this manifestation of the God realm*, too. Let us put our hand in His and run alongside Him with abandon into the mountain ranges of darkness, bringing the light of His glory and ferocious love to answer the call of needy people everywhere.

For the earth will be filled with the knowledge of the glory of the Lord, as the waters cover the sea.

(Habakkuk 2:14)

MANNA AND JEWELS FROM THE GLORY REALM

KAYE BEYER

CHAPTER THREE

How great are His signs, and how mighty His wonders!

(Daniel 4:3 NKJV)

God says that we will see great signs and wonders! He also says, "Jesus Christ is the same yesterday, today and forever" (Hebrews 13:8 NKJV). This means we should expect the miraculous, and the supernatural should be our "natural."

It was only about a year after my husband, Harold, and I were saved (November 11, 1967), that the Lord did an amazing miracle that left us in awe of His greatness and might. Now, almost forty-five years later, as I write this chapter, I am still astounded at God's marvelous works among His people. In 1968, we were living in a small Wisconsin town after we'd accepted Christ's gift of salvation.

As a young married couple trying to find our way in life, we eagerly sought after the things of God and relied on Him to guide us on our journey. We began making mission trips to various countries around the world to help share the Good News. We simply loved Jesus with all of our hearts.

To provide for us, Harold drove a milk truck, transporting raw milk from dairy farmers to the pasteurizing plant in town. He had a special relationship with the Lord and enjoyed wonderful times of prayer and worship each day while driving his routes. Harold spent eight to ten hours a day alone in the truck, and learned to hear the Lord's voice and encountered many special miracles.

A Flaky White Substance

One day, something very unusual happened to Harold while driving his route. When he turned into a farmer's yard, suddenly white crumbs, a flake-like substance, appeared all over his lap. Harold was surprised and had no idea what it was, but he sensed a very strong presence of God with him. As the truck slowed to a stop and he stepped out to load the milk cans, the substance disappeared just as mysteriously as it had appeared.

After he finished loading, Harold got back into the truck to continue with his route. While heading down the driveway to return to the road, to his amazement, the white crumb flakes appeared again all over his lap and on the seat of the truck! This time, God's presence was so heavy that Harold began to weep. He pulled the truck off the road, stopped, and asked the Lord, "What is this?" He heard the Lord say that it was "manna." Then the Lord went on to say that if Harold would serve Him, he would see many signs, wonders, and miracles that other people would not see.

The Lord told Harold that if he would serve Him, he would see many signs, wonders, and miracles that other people would not see.

Harold was in awe of this supernatural manifestation right before his eyes, though he could not help thinking, "No one will ever believe this, but I'll put some manna in my thermos cup and bring it home to show Kaye." However, when he tried to gather it up and place some of it in the thermos cup, it disappeared. Now Harold was very certain he would not tell anyone about this miracle, not even me.

That afternoon when he came home from work and walked through the kitchen door, I took one look at him and saw the glory of the Lord all over him. I knew something had happened, I can't describe it – Harold always had a certain look after an encounter in the glory with the Lord. So, I asked, "What happened today?" He began to tell me about his experience in the milk truck with the white substance, his conversation with the Lord, and his attempt to bring some of the manna home to show me. After hearing everything, I was amazed and excited about what God had done for Harold that day. Even so, I agreed with him that maybe it would be better not to mention it to anyone else, but keep this story between the Lord and us!

It Happens Again

Since it was common for Harold to have various heavenly encounters on the milk route, we thought the appearance of the manna would be a one-time thing. About six months passed and it did not reoccur. Then one evening, when Harold was praying late at night, the manna appeared again. This time it was all over the top of his Bible. Harold was excited – the Lord had sent it again! He rushed into the bedroom and woke me up to come and see it. I could hardly believe my eyes, but it was undeniably there in front of us. We had a great time of rejoicing together in the Lord as His awesome presence filled our home.

We really wanted to share this wonderful experience with someone else, so when we knew our friends Cecil and Blanche Fletcher would be awake, we called them to come over to see the manna. We were all overwhelmed and marveled at this manifestation of God's glory. After a couple of days, it just faded away.

We really did not know if we would ever see it again and wondered what the Lord was doing by giving us this incredible gift. Over the next thirty years, when we would least expect it, there would be the manna. Sometimes it would be a year before we saw it again. Then one cold winter evening, when we were visiting some of our friends, a person who wanted to go home asked us to move our car because it was blocking their car. Harold went out to move it and discovered manna covering his Bible, lying on the front seat. He quickly brought it in the house and we all had a wonderful time of rejoicing. Then we took communion together, using the manna as our bread. We will never forget that night.

There are many stories I could tell about how the manna would appear periodically, and unexpectedly. It was always such a blessing for us and for those who accepted this as a miracle from the Lord. Of course, as with any supernatural manifestation, there were those who did not believe or were skeptical. Sometimes this was disappointing and occasionally hurtful, but we continued to share our testimony and as we did, the Lord brought the manna again and again.

Disbelief and Excommunication

On one occasion, while kneeling and praying at church before the service, when we opened our eyes manna covered both of our Bibles and the pew. By this time, many had heard about the manna but few had seen it. We could not hide it now, and when the people saw it they got excited. At least we thought everyone was excited. However, later on we learned that our pastor had a different point of view. Soon after that incident, the pastor took Harold aside and told him that everything he thought he had gotten from the Lord was actually from the devil.

Finally, they told us that they did not want us to come anywhere near the church. We went through a very difficult three years until we moved to Florida. With no friends in the world and no friends at church, we had no one but Jesus. Yet, when you have Jesus, you have enough. This was a time for us to learn to forgive and go forward, knowing that the Lord was with us. We had not asked for this gift, God gave it to us. Our responsibility was to handle it carefully and make certain to give God all the glory!

One day before work, I was reading and praying when I opened my Bible to Luke where it says, "Daughter … thy faith has made thee whole; go in peace" (Luke 8:48 KJV). Later in the chapter it tells about Jairus' daughter. Jesus came to Jairus' home and told them the girl was sleeping, not dead. The people "laughed him to scorn," but Jesus put them all out except for the parents and three of His disciples. Her spirit came to her again (Luke 8:49-56). I left my Bible open at that passage and went to work.

We had not asked for this gift, God gave it to us. Our responsibility was to handle it carefully and make certain to give God all the glory!

When I returned home that evening, I found manna all over my Bible, especially on the verses about Jairus' daughter who was raised from the dead. Manna was also covering Harold's Bible, lying on the bed. Like that young girl, our spirits came back to us. From that day forward, it no longer mattered to us what anyone said against us. We knew the appearance of the manna was a gift from the Lord and all we needed to do was give Him all the praise and glory for the great things He had done and was doing.

THE "HIDDEN MANNA"

We continued to do mission work and one day while in Venezuela at a pastor's home, the Lord put manna inside our Bibles while they were closed. We found the manna on the Scripture in Revelation 2:17 that says, "To him that overcometh will I give to eat of the hidden manna" (KJV). God poured out His blessings powerfully on that trip and many people were healed and set free as the Lord showed us that the manna He provided could bring healing to those who ate it.

A few years later, around 1998, the manna started to come more frequently. During the next 10 years, the Lord opened doors for us to minister around the world. We gave manna to thousands of people, as we used it for communion bread. After Harold went home to be with the Lord, the Lord gave me the manna one final time, while in Hawaii. There was enough manna to share with more than three hundred people during communion. God is so good. He told me that He is doing a new thing and I should "keep on keeping on," which I have done. The Lord still blesses me with many signs, wonders, and miracles as I travel to minister in many different countries.

The Green Gemstone

One special thing the Lord did for me happened when I was in Idaho a few years ago. I was visiting a friend's home, and they told me about a local couple who had gemstones fall into their front yard. After speaking at a nearby church, we went to see what was going on there. This couple had received many different colors of gems – red, purple, lavender, and diamond-colored – but had never gotten a green stone. However, I did not know that when we arrived. We got out of the car and of course we all started looking around on the ground for gems. After a few minutes, a green stone fell right in front of my feet.

I was beside myself with excitement praising the Lord. When a gem falls from heaven at your feet, you don't sit and wonder if it is the devil or not, you know it is the Lord. What a blessing!

God is getting His bride ready for His return, and the natural always typifies the spiritual. When a bride gets married in the natural, she receives diamonds and jewels from the groom. God is merely sending a few tokens of His affection to let us know how much He loves us. A friend of mine in Hong Kong, who has a jewelry store, set the stone in a ring for me. Now when I minister, I point to it as tangible proof of God's great miracle working power. (The jeweler told us it is fifty carats and flawless.) Praise the Lord!

Our God is indeed a miracle-working God. Miracles are not only for today but God wants to use everyone in miracles, signs, and wonders.
Yes, even YOU!

AN EVENING
WITHOUT GOD

DARREN WILSON

CHAPTER FOUR

Before I made my first film, *Finger of God*, it was fair to say that I was about as "normal" a Christian as you could find. Weird stuff never happened to me, God was firmly stuck in my head and not my heart, and I rarely, if ever, believed any story anyone told about some "experience" they had within the supernatural realm. Of course, if you've seen one of my films, *Finger of God* or *Furious Love*, or read my book, *Filming God*, you'll know that this former skeptic is now a true-blue believer in a God who is very, very active in the world today.

As I highlighted in my first book, a time came when supernatural stuff began to happen to me, which very much tempered my skepticism for other people's wacky stories. Now I was having my own crazy encounters. What follows is a recent "encounter" I had while filming my latest movie, *Father of Lights*.

Something Seriously Wrong

March 6, 2011

Everything was normal until I went to bed. We had arrived in Lubbock, Texas, gotten the rental car, eaten at Chili's, then found our hotel and called it a night. As usual, my right-hand man, Braden, was asleep in seconds (the guy can sleep anywhere, anytime – oh, to be young again) and I closed my eyes to get some shut-eye myself. I quickly realized that I most certainly wasn't going to pass out immediately tonight, so I resorted to my next line of defense against sleepless nights – I started to pray.

Before I start to sound *too* spiritual here, I should probably give full disclosure that I was not praying that the Lord would help me to sleep. That would be far too smart a prayer, and if there is one thing I have made perfectly clear over the years, it's that I'm not always the sharpest spiritual tool in the shed. So instead of praying for the obvious, I figured I would just start to pray *in general,* because surely that would put me to sleep. While I am horrified to admit such thoughts to the general public, I take comfort in the hope that I am not the only person with this unreligious habit. "Can't sleep? Pray! Heck, it put you to sleep in the past because you were so bored doing it; why not try it again?"

So I began to pray, but this time something was wrong. I tried again. Still wrong. I remembered I forgot to set the alarm, so I got out of bed to do that, then snuggled back under the covers and tried again. Still wrong.

What was wrong? Well… I couldn't pray.

Now look, I'm not one of those hocus-pocus types, constantly shoving my tuning fork into the spiritual realm to pick up on every weird wavelength around me. I don't work like that. I have friends (and even some family) who do that, but I'm like a dead fish, most of the time, when it comes to the spiritual realm. God typically has to do a little heavy lifting with me if He wants to get something through my thick spiritual skull.

Digression:

The next day, when I was telling my wife about this episode, the first thing she asked me was, "Do you think there was something that may have been left in the room, something that was trying to torment you?" I gotta admit, that thought never even crossed my mind. I give you this little aside to make clear how naive I was about the utterly strange and nonsensical thing that happened to me in bed that night.

Since when could I not pray? What the heck is going on here? It took me a while to realize that something was seriously wrong. At first I thought my mind was just wandering. I'd say, "Heavenly Father... heavenly Father... heavenly Father..." over and over again but couldn't think of anything else to pray. Then I'd switch to "Dear Jesus... dear Jesus... dear Jesus..." and again, couldn't think of anything more to ask. It was as if there had been some kind of a block placed on my mind, and I was completely incapable of going any further with this prayer.

After a few minutes of this, I began to wonder why I couldn't pray. I remember thinking, "Why can't I pray?" I would try to pray, fail, and then wonder why I couldn't do it. This is important to note for what happened next. And this is when it gets weird...

It was as if a cloud descended over me and I began to have some of the worst thoughts I've had in recent memory. The distance between God and me became more pronounced than it had ever been, and I began struggling with my own insignificance in this world and in the greater cosmos. I was a speck, a flea, in this vast universe.

Then it got worse. I began to doubt my own faith or, at the very least, my own relationship with God. I couldn't even think of anything to pray to Him. I was stuck just saying His name over and over again. I guess I could have asked Him for stuff, but then my depression spiked because I realized that the only thing I could do was ask Him for stuff. Did I really have nothing to say to my King? Was this what our relationship had come to? Or worse, was this really what it had been all along? With me, a petulant child, always approaching God with hat in hand as I begged for a little change, a little help, or a little gift? Could I think of no other way to communicate with Him?

I was lost. Set adrift at sea with no hope of getting back to shore. I had been abandoned or, horror of horrors, there had never been any relationship to begin with. Maybe God wasn't even real. Maybe He was just a figment of my imagination. Maybe my entire life – all my films, all my claims – was built on a foundation of lies and smoke.

I felt this, you see. That is what I have to communicate to you. I felt this stronger than I have felt much else. I was disconnected from Someone I thought I had been connected with. It was as if I had come home to an empty house after ten years of marriage. There were pictures everywhere of me and my wife, but she was gone – so gone that I wondered if she had ever even been there in the first place.

"Dear Jesus… dear Jesus… dear Jesus" – it continued.

"Why can't I pray? Why can't I pray?" – continued.

And then the dream… or vision… or whatever it was, began.

A Dream... or Perhaps a Vision

I was in a backyard, somewhere near my house. I'd never been there before, but it somehow felt familiar. There was a swing set, a seesaw, and a few odds and ends scattered around the yard. And there was my son, Stryder. Six years old and sound asleep. I saw him and knew I had to get him home. It was urgent, I had to get this child home. But he was sleeping, and I didn't want to wake him. I wanted him to remain in peace.

I picked him up and carried him, still asleep, to the road. There was a tricycle there and, as comical as it may seem, I sat down on the tricycle and placed my son on my lap in front of me as I began to pedal down the road. My arms were around him, holding him steady, and I pedaled faster and faster. His big, bushy head was right under my chin and I smelled his hair – put my nose right into his hair – and breathed deeply. My arms tightened around him. And my heart exploded in my chest.

Love!

Love unlike anything I have ever felt before – stronger than my love for

My love for my son was so great I had to expose it to the cos-mos. I had to speak it – simply because it was. "I love you, little buddy ..." And the more I spoke, the more emotion I felt.

my wife or the love I had ever felt for any of my children – burst within me. Love entered my lungs with each breath and surged through my veins to permeate every fiber of my being. As he slept and I pedaled, I began to whisper to him how much I loved him. He couldn't hear me because he was sleeping, but I didn't care – my love for him was so great I had to expose it to the cosmos. I had to speak it – simply because it was. "I love you, little buddy. I love you

so much. You're my pride and joy. You have no idea how much…"
I just kept going, and the more I spoke, the more emotion I felt.

But I had to do more, speaking was not enough – not nearly enough. If you knew me well, you would know how utterly strange my next action truly was. I began to sing over him. I made up songs about my love for him. I let my feelings simply pour from my lips, but inside me the emotions were stronger than any words could possibly describe, or that any song could possibly capture. I cannot tell you the words that I sang, because it was more spirit than song. It was a poem of music for my son, my little boy with the bushy hair. My arms held him tight, and all my thoughts were fixed on him.

I saw the patch of ice ahead but didn't care about it. It was simply ice. It was simply there. The tricycle hit it and began to slide, and I knew immediately that we were going to tip over. I had not seen this happening, my only concern was that my son stay asleep. He need not be concerned with this. I want him to rest. I have to get him home. As the tricycle tipped over, I shielded his body with mine and took the impact. I then got back up, set the tricycle upright again, and we continued on our way.

I arrived home and for some reason had to park the tricycle about 100 feet from the house. I could bike no farther. As soon as I rose from the tricycle with my son still sleeping in my arms, I heard the wolves. They howled and snarled as they came around from behind the house, all three of them. This was no accident. No serendipitous crossing of paths at the same strange moment. They were here for me. They were here for my son. And they were going to attack, whether I liked it or not.

They moved toward us with purpose and ferocity. Their intent was obvious – they were going to tear us limb from limb. They were hungry, ravenous, depraved, and totally evil. They had already advanced beyond the house, and I knew we would never reach the front door in time.

My thoughts at this moment are seared in my mind. There is no question what I was thinking as the wolves closed in. It may have been a dream, but it may as well not have been. It's still so clear – so frightfully clear.

"These wolves will not touch my son."

And then, with not a second thought about it, I raised my son above my head and ran straight toward those wolves. They ran toward me, too, and as they leapt, I knew they were going to utterly destroy me. But they were not going to touch my son.

"Dear Jesus… dear Jesus… dear Jesus"

"Why can't I pray… why can't I pray"

An Awakening

It took me only a few seconds to realize what had just happened. It was as if there had been no pause in my thoughts at all. Whatever had just happened to me (was it a dream, a vision?) had happened seemingly instantaneously, as if it was outside of time.

What did I just dream? With an overwhelming suddenness, every detail came flooding back to me. The tricycle… The ice patch… The wolves… My son… His hair… My embrace… My song… My love!

My God… the love! Even now, the true experience of it was fading as my understanding began to come alive. I cannot understand that kind of love because I was not made to contain it. It is wholly beyond me, beyond what I am capable of. Beyond what I can even *experience*!

I knew instantly what had happened, although I did not yet understand the full significance. I knew I had just experienced something through His eyes, but what exactly? His love for me, certainly. But why? What just happened? One thing was certain, it was nearly midnight and whatever horrible thoughts and feelings I had been feeling before this occurrence were now gone. He was back. I could pray again. I got down to business and, sure enough, was soon sound asleep.

The Morning After

The next day I called my wife to tell her what had happened. After I gave her the details, she asked me when this had taken place. I don't know exactly... around 11pm, I think. She then told me that, oddly enough, she had gone to bed at around 9pm that night (she had just gotten back from two weeks in China and had passed out completely from exhaustion and jet lag). She was inexplicably awkened at 10:30pm and knew, just knew, that she was supposed to pray for me right then. She did so until she fell back asleep at around midnight.

As usual, my wife is the one who connects the dots for me. "Darren, I think God may have been giving you a glimpse of what so many people go through on a daily basis."

As soon as she said that, I knew she was right. The curtain was lifted and the plot was revealed. He had given me a glimpse of the loneliness and disconnect felt by so many of His people. They believe in Him but, whether through circumstances, lack of experience, or their own mind getting in the way, they simply cannot draw near to Him in any meaningful way. What fell on me in that hotel room was not atheism, but distance. The connection had been cut or it had never existed in the first place. Regardless of cause, the truth remained the same. I believed in Him but had no relationship with Him. No friendship. And it was one of the worst feelings in the world.

He showed me what that felt like. I literally couldn't pray. There was nothing to say. What do you say to someone you don't know? It was as if I was dead. No, not dead, because I believed in Him. No, I was asleep.

But then I was Him, and He wanted to show me that even when I couldn't feel Him, couldn't feel His presence, and even wondered if He existed or cared about me at all, my state of mind did not affect His opinion of me one bit. In His eyes, I was simply a sleeping child who would soon wake. But even if I didn't, He was going to lavish His love on me regardless. He was willing to humble Himself (drive a tricycle) as long as it would get me to my destination while He could still hold on to me. And as He held me, He loved me. But He's always holding me, always loving me. And His love is beyond even my capacity to understand it.

And then there are the things that I cannot see while I sleep. A patch of ice that throws me off course; yet He shields me, rights my path, and continues on, His love overpowering even Himself.

He wanted to show me that even when I couldn't feel Him, couldn't feel His presence, and even wondered if He existed or cared about me at all, my state of mind did not affect His opinion of me one bit ... He was going to lavish His love on me.

Then we arrive home – my place of comfort, the place where I belong. It is a place of peace where I may still continue in my slumber but eventually, without question, where I will wake. And once I am awake, I will no longer feel disconnected, because I will be home and my Daddy will be there.

But even as I sleep, the wolves are prowling at my door. They are bent on my destruction, yet I am carried by the Lamb. His only concern is my safety. He doesn't even wake me to tell me to run. These wolves will hurt Him, there is no mistaking that. They will tear into Him and they will relish the fact, because they are wild animals. That's what they do. But they will not touch me because I am His son.

BRAVERY IN A GARDEN

I hear and ponder the concept of God's love for us so much that quite often it loses its potency. So I need to go to witchcraft festivals with my camera or have dreams/visions in my hotel room to be reminded of the awesome nature of that love. But until this dream, I gave very little thought to His bravery. The theology of His sacrifice for me, for all of us, tends to carry with it a sense of inevitability. We read the gospels, knowing what happens in the end. We know He's going to die for us. But I tend to forget that even at the very end, when He was in the garden knowing what He needed to do and why it had to be done, He still asked the Father to make it stop. Being torn apart, being separated from the Father, was His greatest fear.

A dream has made me wonder. How many times have I skimmed over His struggle in the garden as a simple prelude to the main event when, in fact, could the truth possibly be that this moment *was* the main event? Before I am accused of heresy, please hear me out. Obviously our salvation, indeed our friendship with

Him, rests in His death and resurrection. There is no debating that. And, in that sense, His death and resurrection is the defining moment in all history. But when I stared through His eyes at those wolves and knew what they were after, I had a decision to make. Do I make a run for it, try to outrun them? Do I waken the child and try to get him to help me with a diversion? Do I pick up the tricycle and use it as a weapon to fight back?

I imagine Jesus in the garden, His best friends asleep around Him. In a sense, He's all alone. And He knows what's coming. He sees the wolves come out from behind the house and He asks God to take this cup from Him. *Don't make Me do this, Father. Please. It's going to be so painful. It's going to be so awful.* And there is a moment in time, right between those verses of asking for the cup to pass and accepting the will of God, where a very real decision is made. He already knows the answer, but just as God does with us, He must make the decision Himself.

We are in His arms at that moment. We are asleep. We don't know what is going on around us. We are unaware of the danger we are in. And it is that moment, the moment of bravery beyond all bravery, before or since, that our fates are decided by our Father and our Friend. When He gives His will for life over to the Father, that's the moment when He raises us high above His head and charges after the wolves, not to fight them but to give them exactly what they want.

They can have Him, but they cannot have us.

Hug Your Father

As I pondered all this, I was filled with gratitude and love for a Daddy like this. But I also felt a pain of sadness that He gets to put His arms around me, yet I cannot do the same to Him. He is Spirit, and unless He chooses to show Himself to me in the flesh, I am stuck trying to give Him a purely spiritual hug. I want to embrace Him, but it's like hugging a cloud. I want something physical. I'm sick of the spiritual, I'm sick of those limitations. *God, it's not fair. Why can You hug me, feel me in Your arms, but I cannot do the same with You?*

The answer was immediate and as clear as it was obvious.

"You can hug Me whenever you want. Where did I tell you to find Me? In the poor… The brokenhearted… The downtrodden… The widows… The orphans… The hungry… The lost… I am always available for an embrace, a physical one at that, but it seems you very rarely want what you say you want. You can have dinner with Me whenever you like. You can feed Me whenever you like. You can honor Me with gifts whenever you like. I am all around you."

A Violent Love

If Jesus is our great example, then He gives us yet another example of how to react when we feel disconnected from Him, or we disagree with Him, or we feel like He's allowing things to happen to us that He shouldn't be allowing. After all, He's God, He can do whatever He wants. All it takes to heal us or to heal our kids is for Him to snap His fingers and it's done. He's done it for others, why not for us? Why is He making us go through this? Why isn't He bailing us out? Why is He allowing this to happen? Why isn't He talking to us? Why does He feel so distant?

At the risk of using a cheap phrase, *what would Jesus do?* What did He do? When faced with the greatest pain and disconnect in history, did He wallow in His misery? Certainly He cried. Certainly He had His evening of intense stress and questioning. But even as His friends scattered, leaving Him utterly alone, He walked into the wolves for us. He went by Himself, holding us up high so they could never get us again. In the midst of His own struggle, His thoughts turned to us, to others. Even as He underwent the great disconnect, He looked outward and He loved others violently.

Is God not talking to you? Do you feel disconnected from His presence? Are you upset that He's allowing something, or that He allowed something to happen that you think He should have stopped? Are you mad at Him? Bewildered by Him? Growing up, I always heard Christians talk about "seasons." This is a testing season, or a healing season, or a desert season. I'm starting to think there are only two seasons: awake or asleep. When you're awake, you feel His presence, you enjoy His companionship, or you've got a flowing, communicative relationship with Him. Yet when you're asleep, for whatever reason (yes, maybe He put you to sleep), you may not feel Him. But He holds you tight, His head buried in your hair, singing over you as He takes you home where, soon enough, you will awaken from your slumber and Daddy will be there. And it will be time to start your next adventure together.

> The Lord your God in your midst,
>
> The Mighty One, will save;
>
> He will rejoice over you with gladness,
>
> He will quiet you with His love,
>
> He will rejoice over you with singing.
>
> (Zephaniah 3:17 NKJV)

JESUS ENCOUNTERS IN THE SUPERNATURAL

STACEY CAMPBELL

CHAPTER FIVE

God is on the move. In every nation, I hear of great miracles and signs that He is performing. A couple of months ago, I was in Brazil speaking at a conference. A young woman came up to me at the end of my session to ask me to pray for her mother who had just been in an automobile accident. She was desperate because her mother was hovering between life and death. As we bowed our heads to pray, the story of the Roman centurion who asked Jesus to heal his servant came to mind:

> And when Jesus entered Capernaum, a centurion came to Him, imploring Him, and saying, "Lord, my servant is lying paralyzed at home, fearfully tormented." Jesus said to him, "I will come and heal him." But the centurion said, "Lord, I am not worthy for You to come under my roof,

but just say the word, and my servant will be healed. For I also am a man under authority, with soldiers under me; and I say to this one, 'Go!' and he goes, and to another, 'Come!' and he comes, and to my slave, 'Do this!' and he does it" (Matthew 8: 5-9).

The Holy Spirit fell on me, and I began shaking and decreeing aloud, "God is in the hospital room with your mother, the same as He is with us now. And He is listening to our prayers and can heal her right now!" So, with great faith, we began to command life into her body.

The next day, the young woman returned to the conference and gave me a report: "My mother was hanging between life and death yesterday. She could see in the spirit that the sky opened over her and a great host of demonic faces encircled her and her spirit was being pulled out of from her body. Suddenly, in the middle of that demonic circle, she saw a woman with blonde hair appear, shaking her head. As the woman shook her head, the dying woman watched the demons flee and her spirit flew back into her body. She was completely healed of everything except her broken collarbone" (go figure). The daughter went on to say her mother would be discharged from the hospital right away.

Every week, I see or hear of extraordinary miracles. They encourage me to continually press into God. Yet, the most impacting encounters I have are when He speaks to me directly. I have not had this happen many times, but every time I hear the audible voice of God, it is life changing. The voice of God carries such authority and so many layers of revelation that a few words from Him create more impact than reading a hundred books.

The experiences I will share are personal – God's dealings with me – but I pray that through them you will discover how deeply

God cares about your personal life, your divine destiny, and discover how He is working to bring about His good pleasure in you. He helps us in our weaknesses and leads us out of darkness into His marvelous light (1 Peter 2:9).

First Encounter

My first vision of God in the glory realm happened when I was a child; long before I knew Him, He knew me. This is a profound truth because we are not a random coincidence evolved over time on a planet hidden within a plethora of galaxies. We were each individually created in the image of God, and we are completely known by the One who wants to be known by us. Therefore, He searches for us before we ever search for Him. This is why Scripture says that we can only love Him because He first loved us (1 John 4:19).

This encounter is why I became a genuine seeker of God. When I was a child, about six or seven years old, I had my first vision of Jesus. I had been to a vacation Bible school in my tiny village in rural Saskatchewan, Canada. The Bible school teacher had told the story of children coming to Jesus, and I vividly remembered those flannel-graph pictures of Him. "How kind He looks," I thought with my child's mind. The story drew me and gave me an overwhelming desire to see Jesus, to climb into His lap as the children in the story did. The story so affected me that I prayed before going to sleep that night, "Jesus, I want to see you. Can I please see you like the other kids saw you?" The Lord answered my prayer that very night in a dream.

As I slept, Jesus appeared to me. However, He was nothing like the flannel-graph Jesus. Instead of His kindness, I felt the glory of His majesty. Although He was huge, immense, gigantic, when He appeared directly in front of me, I recognized Him instantly.

Remembering how He had allowed the children to come to Him, I began racing in His direction.

As I ran, however, He began to speak and His voice was like thunder booming not only outside but also inside me. Instantly, I was overcome with dread. I stopped running, fell on my face, and covered my head with my hands to protect myself from the raw power of His being. His words were simple: "Christ has died; Christ is risen; *Christ will come again!*" They were simple but unforgettable words with an emphasis clearly on the final phrase: *"CHRIST WILL COME AGAIN!"*

The image of Jesus and the echo of that thundering voice have never left me. Though I was very young and did not understand it at the time, that one encounter changed my whole life. From that moment on, I knew that God was real, that He was powerful, and that He was coming again. I innately understood that He deeply cared that I do good and not evil. Since that experience, as though by impartation, I have had a clear understanding of the difference between right and wrong. That one dream birthed in me a discerning conscience, which has deterred me from many sins and encouraged me to search for God in every season of my life. I received a gift from seeing Jesus that night: an impartation of the "fear of the Lord."

I felt the glory of His majesty. He was huge, immense, gigantic. His voice was like thunder booming not only outside but also inside me. I fell on my face, and covered my head with my hands to protect myself from the raw power of His being. His words were simple: "Christ has died; Christ is risen; *Christ will come again!*"

Many prophets in the Bible have been gripped with a fear of the Lord at the beginning of their ministries (see Isaiah 6:5; Ezekiel 1:28; 2:6; Jeremiah 1:6-8; Jonah 1:3). What many do not understand when they read these accounts, however, is that the deeper outcome of "visions of God" (Ezekiel 1:1) is longing. Although the dream I had was shocking, particularly taking into account my young age, the imprint of God remained, and after I saw Him that one time, the thing I wanted most was more of Him. Now I knew that He was actually there and that He was not silent or uninvolved with my world and with me.

My problem was that I did not know how to find Him again. I was in an environment that did not encourage Bible reading. Although I continued to pray nightly, it would be many years before I had another supernatural encounter. Yet, I could not get rid of the desire to know God. In fact, the desire created by that initial impartation remains with me today and compels me to pursue Him… no matter what the cost.

My Second Encounter in the God Realm

My early experience was foundational to my personal pursuit of Jesus. It ignited a flame in my heart to know God. It was for me, "the beginning of wisdom," and the fear of the Lord guided my decisions for years. However, it would be a long time before I encountered God again. Other than a few demonic attacks and a couple of vivid dreams, I did not have any further supernatural encounters until my second year of university.

As was my custom, every night before bed, I took out my Bible and began to pray it, slowly and meditatively, verse by verse. One evening, I was praying through the book of Isaiah and I was at chapter 40:15-18:

Surely the nations are like a drop in a bucket; they are regarded as dust on the scales; he weighs the islands as though they were fine dust. Lebanon is not sufficient for altar fires, nor its animals enough for burnt offerings. Before him all the nations are as nothing; they are regarded by him as worthless and less than nothing. With whom, then, will you compare God? To what image will you liken him?

Suddenly, my whole room lit up with a golden glow...

A holy Presence filled the room. Tears began falling from my eyes onto my open Bible. I felt my spirit being lifted out of my body and the next thing I knew, I was flying over the nations with the Lord by my side.

Like a view from the space shuttle, I could see entire continents at first, then nations and cities. Sometimes we zoomed in on certain countries and God would reveal to me His sovereignty over everything in that country (Psalm 24:1, 2). Occasionally, we even landed at nations that were at war or in a conflict. When we did, I was filled with understanding that, even in difficult circumstances where men had rebelled against Him, God could make everything work together for our good and His purposes (Romans 8:28).

Nothing fazed Him; He was aware of everything going on and showed me what He saw and, in part, how He saw things. There was no question – He was ultimately over and above all nations. I received a clear and unmistakable view of God's sovereignty over all things. As the Lord returned my spirit to my body, I heard His voice say, "I AM Lord of the nations. And I AM Lord of you. And I want you to ..."

The next thing I knew I was flying over the nations with the Lord by my side. I received a clear and unmistakable view of God's sovereignty over all things. As the Lord returned my spirit to my body, I heard His voice say, "I AM Lord of the nations. And I AM Lord of you."

That was when He gave me clear instructions about what I was to do with my life. He seemed to know that I would not do what He wanted without these instructions, because following them would require a very high personal cost. I knew that I could say "yes" or "no," because he prefaced the instructions with "I *want* you to ..." It was not a demand, but an expression of the desire of the heart of God for my life.

A Theocentric Shift

My entire future was set in motion from that experience. I had what I call "a theocentric shift," meaning that from that "out of body" encounter, I understood that I was created for a divine destiny (Ephesians 2:10). My life was not my own; I was bought with a price (1 Corinthians 6:20; 7:23). I also knew that I could choose to do His will or follow my own plans. In hindsight, I cannot express how glad I am that I chose God's plan over my own. The wisdom of His ways continues to astound me.

These initial experiences put a high standard within me. They helped me to navigate my choices and led me in the ways of God. However, in my immature understanding of grace, I placed the same high standards on everyone around me. As a result, I became critical of the sins of others. I had a heightened awareness of right and wrong, but a low tolerance for people who did not "measure up." Sadly, my critical heart intensified as I grew older, especially toward other believers. I felt that believers should "know better," so when fellow Christians struggled with sin, I could not understand their dilemma. I easily understood truth but did not understand mercy – that is, until I needed it myself.

During my first year of marriage and my third year of university, I walked into the restroom at a Christian gathering and saw someone throwing up in the toilet. Rather than question this behavior, a lie entered my mind. I could literally feel something jump onto my head, and I found myself thinking, "That's a good idea. I'm gaining weight lately. I should do that." From that day, I became severely bulimic, throwing up several times a day. This behavior continued for about eight months, progressively increasing until it consumed my life. I knew it was wrong, but I couldn't seem to help myself. I became depressed, even suicidal, thinking that God was angry with me because "I should know better."

He encompassed me with waves of unconditional love. Then He said, "If you do that till the day you die, I will still love you."

When Jesus came to me in an open vision, I was undone. He encompassed me with waves of unconditional love. Then He said, "If you do that till the day you die, I will still love you." I was instantly healed, and I learned how God sees people with love, even when they sin. That understanding changed the way I view people and how I prophesy.

THE FELLOWSHIP OF HIS SUFFERING

Possibly the most powerful experience I ever had from a direct encounter with Jesus, however, was sensing the "flashes of fire" of the jealousy of God (Song of Solomon 8:6). I was about 36 years old when this happened, and it is the deepest experience I've ever had with the Lord. However, this encounter resulted from a prayer I had been praying for several months.

Again, as was my custom, I had been praying verse by verse through the book of Philippians prior to this experience. After a few months, I arrived at chapter 3, verse 10: "… that I may know Him and the power of His resurrection and *the fellowship of His sufferings*, being conformed to His death" (Phillipians 3:10).

The first time I read this verse, the middle part jumped off the page, "That I may know Him *and the fellowship of His sufferings*." What an intriguing concept I thought! How could Paul – and how could I – fellowship with the sufferings of Christ? I had no idea what it meant. How could I know God and fellowship with His sufferings? I reasoned that this was a post-cross and post-resurrection verse by the time Paul prayed it, meaning that Paul was not fellowshipping with the physical sufferings of Christ.

When Paul prayed this verse, Jesus had already descended into the lower parts of the earth, ascended far above all the heavens (Ephesians 4:8-10) and was already seated at the right hand of God (Mark 16:19; Acts 2:33; 7:55, 56). Yet, Paul asked to know God in the *fellowship of His sufferings*. How could Jesus be suffering in His resurrected state? What would make Him suffer even though He was with His Father in heaven?

I could not think of any answer to this question, but I began to pray Paul's prayer anyway. I remember being afraid to pray it at first. Thinking of the physical sufferings of Christ, where many "were appalled at Him [because] His appearance was so disfigured beyond that of any human being and His form marred beyond human likeness" (Isaiah 52:14). My mind began to envision the worst. I remembered reading *Foxe's Book of Martyrs* and thought of the testimonies from Chinese Christians who had been tortured, so I actually expected some physical suffering to result from praying this prayer.

However, my desire to know all of God, even the fellowship of His sufferings, was greater than my fear of pain, so I continued to pray it nightly. Day after day for about eight months, I prayed this apostolic prayer: "Jesus, I want to know what makes You suffer as You pray for us. I want to fellowship with You in that suffering. I want to know You in that place where You experience pain. Cause me to know and experience You in this way."

Though I anticipated some terrible tragedy would befall me, none did. In fact, the opposite happened. Renewal and revival broke out in Toronto and all over the world. Wesley and I found our ministry exploding and we began to travel extensively as a result. Because our children were small, we decided that we would be part of the revival as a family, meaning we would take our children with us. So, we began to travel up to ten months a year, with our small children (aged 7, 3, 1, and 1 month old when we started). Everywhere we went, the Holy Spirit was falling as God touched thousands of people. The gifts and power of the Spirit were breaking out – prophecy, healing, and salvation by the hundreds and thousands in many nations.

FLASHES OF FIRE

Our lives were like characters from the era of the Great Awakening or the Welsh Revival. In many ways, it was absolutely glorious. However, the ministry expansion also brought with it great personal challenges. We had to leave our home and often moved every three days to a new city... and another meeting. We had to leave everything that was familiar behind, including our friends and family. We lived with our five small children in tiny hotel rooms or the homes of virtual strangers. I homeschooled the children, while preaching and prophesying at three services a day.

It was not long until I was physically exhausted, but there was no time to slow down. The meetings were booked months in advance and each venue was packed with hungry people seeking God. Wesley and I took turns preaching and watching the kids and in addition, I prophesied for hours each day. I was still nursing the baby, so I was also awake several times a night in addition to my grueling daily schedule. The more tired I got, the more stressed I became.

The stress primarily affected my personal relationships. Because we were gone for months at a time, the church we founded and pastored felt abandoned. As a result, when we did go home after weeks or months on the road, we had many extra meetings just to catch up – most of which were filled with conflict. Wesley and I also began experiencing strife in our marriage.

Stress was increasing day by day and the conflict between my personal life and my "pulpit life" was a source of much spiritual pain. I was so tired that when I tried to spend time with the Lord, I usually just fell asleep. One day when feeling completely overwhelmed and very sorry for myself, I looked up at the ceiling, with tears running down my face, I said to God, "This is too much for me."

At that moment, I felt a flash of fire go through not only my body, but also every part of my soul and spirit. The fire separated the pure from the impure inside me (see Hebrews 4:12). I cannot describe it adequately, but that flash of lightening or fire filled me with a new revelation, and I could see motivations in my heart that I had never been aware of before.

Then I heard the audible voice of God… And His tone was stern. The rebuke from the mouth of God was unquestionable, He stated, "YOU ASKED FOR IT!" As He spoke these words, He reminded me of my prayer, "That I may know You and the fellowship of Your sufferings." Then, in what seemed like a millisecond, He went through the prayers I had prayed all my life, especially highlighting one that I prayed many times: "Lord, You can have everything in my life, EXCEPT please don't take Wesley." I honestly felt that I could not live without Wesley. That flash of jealous fire exposed my co-dependence.

God showed me how much my "EXCEPT" prayer hurt Him. He is a jealous God. He does not want to be second to anyone or anything – not father, mother, son, daughter, or even your husband (Matthew 10:37-39). I went from tears of self-pity to sobbing in remorse for how much I had hurt the heart of God for years. It was true – I did ask for it and I fellowshipped with Him in the pain of His jealousy. For three days, I could hardly stop sobbing. The "Person of God" pierced me more than any time before or since. God does not want to be second to anything in our lives – not our careers, our bank accounts, our homes, our lifestyles, our families, or relationships. Because He is in love with us, He is jealous over the affections of our hearts. He wants us to love Him *first*.

All of my encounters in the glory realm have led me closer to God. They made the Bible come alive and deepened my understanding of the heart and mind of God.

Here is what I hope you take away from this chapter:

- God is not merely a flannel-graph figure who bounces children on His knee like a doting grandfather. He IS our loving heavenly Father but He is so much more – an awesome all-powerful Being who created us for a purpose and Who deserves our love, respect, and yes – even our fear.

- The world, its kingdoms, and its leaders do not intimidate God. He is at work, making even the appalling things that occur, because of satan's intervention and human greed and lust for power, work together for our good and His plan to redeem humanity.

- He has a part for each of us to play in bringing His Kingdom to earth.

- We wound the heart of God with the things we place ahead of Him. He put us first, even over His Son's welfare and comfort, and He wants us to put Him first in our hearts, too!

Knowing God is our ultimate destiny (John 17:3) and divine encounters set our hearts on fire to love Him in the way He wants us to love Him and to love others as He does.

HEALINGS AND MIRACLES IN THE GLORY

JOAN HUNTER

CHAPTER SIX

I hope that reading accounts of God's healing power will fill you with faith that God can heal you and use you to heal others. He can and He will astound you with His love and power when you act in faith and pray for the sick. God wants to collaborate with you to display His glory on the earth. Matthew 16 makes it clear that Jesus gave His disciples the power and authority to pray for the sick and see them recover:

> I will give you the keys of the kingdom of heaven; and whatever *you* bind on earth shall have been bound in heaven, and whatever *you* loose on earth shall have been loosed in heaven (Matthew 16:19 emphasis added).

You too can be an agent of God's miracle-working power, not just a passive observer, watching a sick and dying world pass before your eyes. God is constantly displaying His love in new ways, each more astonishing than the last. God is releasing a new wave of healing and glory in this season. Now is the time for us to stay in a place of faith, pray for the sick, and watch as the glory of God descends in signs and wonders.

Being involved in the ministry of healing for more than 40 years has been a great blessing. I have co-pastored a church, traveled around the world with my parents, Charles and Frances Hunter, and now lead my own ministry and author books on healing. I have ministered healing before crowds of several hundred-thousand and groups of less than fifty. Every healing – whether a life-threatening situation, relatively minor problem, or merely an annoying condition, whether the healing is completed instantaneously, or over time – is a miraculous release of God's power and love.

A healing causes all who know about it to praise God and celebrate His goodness. That is why every healing is a "sign and wonder" – a "sign" of God's love and a "wonder" for all who witness it.

A healing causes all who know about it to praise God and celebrate His goodness. That is why every healing is a "sign and wonder" – a "sign" of God's love and a "wonder" for all who witness it.

BREAD, YES! FORMULAS, NO

God always intended healing to be "the children's bread," not a last resort (see Matthew 15:26-27). By using the word "bread," Jesus indicated that healing should be as natural as eating for God's children. It should be a normal, everyday occurrence in the church – not an event that happens once in a lifetime. The four Gospels and Acts are full of stories of healings, and the power of God to heal today is as great now as it was then.

No matter how many times I see God heal, I am still amazed. He never ceases to astound me with the many ways that He heals people. He is certainly not limited to doing anything in only one manner. Some Christians believe that God can only heal at church on Sunday or when the elders come together to anoint the sick with oil. However, Jesus rarely healed anyone in a synagogue and we don't know of Him anointing anyone with oil. God is infinitely creative in all His ways. Some look for healing formulas to put their trust in, but God requires that our faith be in Him as the Healer, not in some method. His love always surprises us! I want to share with you some of the more unusual healings I have experienced that don't fit into anyone's formula:

One night I found it very difficult to sleep. I dozed all night, but was never able to fall into a deep, restful sleep. The next morning when I got out of bed, I was tired and felt as if I had not slept but had worked all night. Two weeks later, a woman called the office to thank me for coming to Northern Ireland to pray for her healing. She had been in a hospital bed in Northern Ireland, crying out to God, asking Him to send me to her hospital room to pray for her. Her condition was desperate and her doctors had told her she might not have long to live.

She was certain that if I came there to pray for her, she would be healed. The very night I had tossed and turned, unable to rest, someone touched her head and awakened her. When she opened her eyes, I was standing next to her bed, praying over her and then she was dramatically healed. Praise God! Although I had not been there physically, God answered her prayer in a unique way.

Several years ago, I was at an international convention for Christian business people when a woman approached me. She thanked me repeatedly for coming to Benin to minister healing to her people. At that time, I didn't even know there was a nation named Benin! She and a group of women at this convention told me they had seen me with their own eyes ministering there at a meeting even though I knew I had never been there! I couldn't even spell Benin at that time. God is ever faithful and always amazing! Many times during my mother's (Frances Hunter) ministry, similar things happened. People saw her pray for the sick in hospitals and other places that she never actually visited physically... and they were healed.

Healing Angels

On a number of occasions, my ministry team members and I have had visions of body parts flowing into people who needed a miracle. During a meeting several years ago, I saw angels appear as I was speaking, each carrying a different type of backpack. When I prayed for people, the angels would reach into their packs and toss something at the person needing healing. As this continued, I came to realize they were hurling body parts into each person! I clearly saw a spine enter into a person with a bad back. Later, in the same meeting, I saw a kidney fly across the room and enter another person. Every time this happened, the person who received a body part would stagger backward as if they had been pushed. Since the first time this happened, I have experienced this on many occasions. Every time it has occurred, the person was immediately and completely healed!

Some of my staff members have had similar experiences. When healing angels show up, they manifest themselves in powerful and dramatic ways. In the past, some of my staff members have been reluctant to pray for healing over the phone, because they thought they did not have the same anointing for healing I have. One day a female staff person received a call from a woman in Canada with a back problem. Although the lady was hesitant for anyone other than me to pray for her, she finally agreed to allow the staff person to try. While praying, she had a vision of a spine going into the phone and down the telephone wire to the woman on the other end of the call. Suddenly, the woman cried out in surprise and joy because she had received a new spine and was now pain free! Thank You, Jesus!

What God does through me, He can do through you or any believer. God is the Healer – we are merely conduits for His love and power. Jesus is the Anointed One. I am merely His servant, as are you. All that you and I are required to do is *pray* for the sick, it is God's job to *heal* them... and He will!

Rods and Plates Evaporate

It has been such a blessing to watch as God performs unexpected miracles. One type of miracle that never ceases to amaze me is the healing of people who have had metal surgically placed in their bodies. Some have had artificial hip or knee replacements,

What God does through me, He can do through you or any believer. God is the Healer – we are merely conduits for His love and power. Jesus is the Anointed One. I am merely His servant, as are you. All that you and I are required to do is *pray* for the sick, it is God's job to *heal* them... and He will!

and others have plates or rods put in their ankles and elsewhere. It is not unusual for God to remove all the surgically implanted metal at the same time He heals.

Perhaps the most impressive example of this type of healing is when those who have had their vertebrae fused and titanium rods implanted are healed. When you have this type of procedure, you cannot bend over very far. However, I have been blessed to watch thousands of people with metal rods or fusions in their backs healed, become pain free and are able to touch their toes. I remember one man in particular who had suffered 15 back operations to fuse most of his vertebrae and had two metal rods implanted in his back. In spite of all those procedures, he was in great pain. His doctors had no answers and told him to learn to live with the pain.

He hobbled slowly as he came forward for prayer, but afterward he was able to run up and down the steps of the platform without pain or assistance. I asked him to check how far he could bend over and he discovered to his delight that he could easily touch his toes without pain! (You can't do that with metal rods in your back.) We have seen this same thing occur in people who had artificial hips, knees, and metal plates located in various places in their bodies. God is still "able to do exceedingly abundantly above all that we ask or think, according to the power that works in us" (Ephesians 3:20 NKJV).

THE GREATEST HINDRANCE TO HEALING

There is *nothing* our God can't do, but He usually chooses to act in response to the actions, faith, and prayers of His people. Our job is to pray in faith for the sick – it is His job to heal them. Unfortunately, fear of failure keeps most Christians from ever praying for the sick. When you wonder, "What will happen if I pray for

God is still "able to do exceedingly abundantly above all that we ask or think, according to the power that works in us."

them and they are not healed?" you are taking responsibility for the sick person's healing. You cannot heal anyone – it is God's "power that works in us" (HE does the work) and once you *really* grasp that truth you will discover a new freedom from the fear of failure.

Healing is like salvation in that only God can save a soul, we can't. However, if we allow ourselves to become discouraged when someone rejects the gospel, we will soon stop sharing this most important truth with those who need it most. In the same way, those who need healing may never receive it if we allow fear or discouragement, due to lack of results previously, to keep us from praying for them.

To live successfully in the glory, we must learn that every aspect of Christianity has both natural and supernatural elements. As we trust and obey, He acts to save and heal. When we co-labor with Him, we will see a supernatural outcome. When we act as if our own abilities are the key to a supernatural outcome we will see few results and quickly become discouraged. However, when we realize it is all in His capable hands, we are released to act and speak in confidence, knowing that He is totally responsible to save, heal, and manifest His glory on the earth.

U-Turn Healings and Astonishing Miracles

There are times when the anointing to heal is so powerful that people just standing in line, waiting for prayer, are healed. This happens so frequently that we refer to them as U-Turn healings.

They come to the prayer line in pain, suddenly discover their conditions have vanished without hands-on ministry, and return to their seats praising God!

It is also common for people sitting in the congregation to be healed while there is prayer for someone with a similar condition. One woman needed a new thyroid and received it as I prayed for another woman whose thyroid had been surgically removed. Both women were healed instantly and received new thyroids! When people watch others with a comparable condition being healed, they reach out to God in faith and are often healed without receiving ministry. Thank You, Jesus!

Creative miracles are always wondrous. I've prayed for victims of rectal cancer many times. After I prayed for one woman whose rectum had been surgically removed, she went to the bathroom to check herself and returned to the meeting rejoicing. God had given her a new rectum. Another creative miracle occurred as I prayed for a woman with an open wound. A man in the congregation began rubbing his leg. He had been born without a calf muscle in one leg. As I prayed for the woman, God gave him a new calf muscle! The woman's open wound closed up at the same time.

Another form of creative miracle sometimes takes place when I minister to women who have been sexually promiscuous earlier in their lives. When they repent of their sexual sins, asking God to remove covenants made through sexual unions and asking Him to restore their purity, He sometimes gives them a new hymen. Later, when they get married, the new hymen breaks on their wedding night. God is so amazing!

A different but equally incredible creative miracle occurred one day, as I prayed for a woman with terrible cataracts. After prayer, she wiped her eyes and the milky cataracts literally came off on her fingers! Her vision was totally restored and she went her way rejoicing in the Lord. We have also seen many breasts grow back. One woman, who was pushed out of a window and landed on her chest, lost both of her breasts; another had a breast burned off as a child, and several had lost their breasts due to mastectomies – but all were healed by our loving God.

YOU HAVE A POCKETFUL OF MIRACLES

Scripture says:

These signs will accompany those who have believed: in My name they will cast out demons, they will speak with new tongues; they will pick up serpents, and if they drink any deadly poison, it will not hurt them; *they will lay hands on the sick, and they will recover* (Mark 16:17-18 emphasis added).

Are you a believer? Then you qualify to release God's glory on the earth through miracles, signs, and wonders. "Signs will accompany" you everywhere you go — all you have to do is dispense them by putting your faith into action and praying for the sick. As you release your faith and God confirms your words, the healing power of God will go into them and they will be healed, because you will have focused His glory on their needs. As people are healed, others will see and glorify God for what He has done. In addition, you will be blessed and filled with joy as God partners with you to bring the glory of His Kingdom to your corner of the earth.

God's love and power to heal really have no limits, other than our faith. Put your faith into action today!

BRANDED BY THE
FIRE OF LOVE

GEORGIAN BANOV

CHAPTER SEVEN

Growing up in Bulgaria during the communist regime was very difficult. The government controlled our lives and dominated us by fear; everyone knew that saying the wrong thing could land you in prison or even get you killed. At a very tender age, I knew more about human poverty and degrading treatment than anyone should. Cut off from the outside world, daily we were indoctrinated with lies. The government took over our family's property and took away our rights of ownership for the "good of the state," and our leaders made certain that we were brainwashed to be good atheists.

Before I was born, all of our Bibles had been collected and publicly burned; even their printing plates were destroyed. I never heard the Scriptures while growing up, and I never even heard the Lord's name spoken aloud. Consequently, we did not know anything about God, because we were made to believe that there was no God.

ROCK STAR

When "rock and roll" music hit Western Europe in the mid 1960s, I discovered the Beatles by secretly listening to illegal broadcasts on my grandfather's shortwave radio. I was a classically trained musician, and this new music was unlike anything I had ever heard. Captivated by the strange but wonderful new sounds, I shared this forbidden pleasure with three of my musician friends and it ignited the fire of our youthful passion. We formed the first official rock band of Bulgaria. In 1965, we made our debut on national television to become an overnight sensation. Rock music became the vehicle through which we could rebel and vent our frustration. Young people came to our concerts in droves, finding out about them by word of mouth.

The communists never saw it coming but soon the clapping, shouting masses deeply frightened them. Rock and roll began to smell like the beginnings of a revolution and before long they pulled the plug on us. The government outlawed our music and they banned our public concerts. This pushed me beyond my limits of tolerance for my lack of personal freedom. There was no way that I could return to the colorless life that the communists had plotted out for me.

Even though it meant risking my life, I rashly decided to escape to the Western world. It all happened very fast and I had to pinch myself to believe I was actually being smuggled across the Iron Curtain through a secret black market route. The next thing I knew, I was on board an American airplane, flying over the Atlantic Ocean, heading for the land of the free.

After landing in New York, my heart was set on pursuing rock and roll; I was eager to go to Hollywood where I thought the action was. Because I arrived with no money, it took me a full year to make my way across the United States. First, I worked in Florida, digging ditches during the day and washing dishes at night. Then I went to Detroit where I worked on an automobile assembly line. Finally, I had just enough money to make my way out to California. Little did I know that the God I did not believe in was waiting for me there.

CALIFORNIA DREAMIN'

Even though I was now living in a free country, somehow I did not feel free yet and I couldn't quite understand why. I was pursuing my dreams, looking for something beautiful, but I didn't know what it was exactly. I was certain that freedom of expression was one of the pieces to the puzzle but other than that I had no idea what I was looking for. I figured that I would recognize "it" when I found it.

With this frame of mind, I met some young hippies on the streets of Ojai, California, who were real "Jesus freaks." This was at the end of the Jesus movement in the early '70s and there was a revival among many young people at that time. This group in particular was out on the streets every day, sharing the joy and peace they had found in Jesus. They also ran a house for people recovering from drug and alcohol abuse.

Every time I saw them, they said things like "Jesus loves you, He really does," and "He died for you!" I remember thinking, "What kind of drug are they on?" They would smile and look at me with "dreamy" stares – at times, I could actually see *something* leaking from their eyes. Later on, I would understand that God's

joy, peace, and love was pouring out of their eyes and radiating ir-
resistibly in the frequencies of their voices.

Through a word of wisdom they realized, *hey – this Bulgarian
guy is really hungry and we should feed him!* I may have been a total
atheist but I was also broke and always famished. They invited me
to dinner at their house. I went with them, the food was great, and
I ate tons!

They invited me to come and eat with them the next day. I
certainly did not believe in anything they were talking about but
I was happy to join them to eat a good meal – I quickly accepted
their invitation.

Good Food, Bad Music

Once they learned that I was a professional musician, they
pulled out their instruments and began playing their music for me.
I was astounded, but not in a good way. All of their guitars, their
piano, and their flute were all painfully out of tune. As they played,
I was thinking, *what is wrong with them, don't they even notice how
bad they sound?* It drove me nuts. I was cringing inside hoping that
they would stop and take a tuning break. To make matters worse,
all of their songs used only three chords (C, D, and G) and they
rotated between these three chords all night long.

I thought, *they should be crying right now after playing such pa-
thetic music, yet they are so excited, acting like they are playing to
a crowd in a sold-out stadium.* They did not seem to notice my
reaction because they were completely lost in their music. I, on
the other hand, was wondering what was wrong with this picture.
With my musical background and knowledge, I sat there feeling
completely miserable, but they were filled with so much joy and

happiness. When they finally finished, they put down their instruments and asked, "So what did you think, Georgian?"

I desperately wanted to say, "Seriously? Give me whatever drug you are on that makes you feel good for no reason, and I want it right now!" Instead, I mumbled something just to be polite. After all, dinner was about to be served. They were persistent in reminding me at every opportunity, "Jesus loves you" and continued inviting me to dinner every day.

> I desperately wanted to say, "Give me whatever drug you are on that makes you feel good for no reason, and I want it right now!"

Every day I would think, *Endure all of that just for a free meal? No way!* However, by six o'clock the hunger pains would hit, and I would find myself back in their house listening to really bad music just so I could fill my belly with their good food. After two months, I finally said to myself, *I can't do this anymore. I don't believe a word of what they are saying about this Jesus, I'm just eating their food. It's time to go down to Hollywood and get on with my business of becoming a rock star. But first, just in case there is some truth in what they're telling me, I'll give it one chance.*

Experience on the Mountain

To be alone, I headed to the nearest mountain. Unsure of what to do or say, my mind was going crazy: *What are you doing? How can you talk to someone that you don't believe is there? This is so stupid; I don't know what to say!*

Then unexpectedly, a question came to me – God, do You exist? *Great,* I thought, *you know He doesn't, but go ahead, say it and get it over with.* So, alone on that mountaintop, I said it aloud, certain that no one could hear me… "God, do You exist?"

KA-BOOM! As soon as I uttered those words, everything changed. I was stunned. I could feel someone or something all around me, and as a musician I could sense that even the acoustics of the mountain air had changed.

The presence that surrounded me became thicker and more palpable, and I began to shake.

"What is happening?" I cried out. The more that I talked, the thicker this presence became. Suddenly, the revelation that God actually exists ran through me like a lightning bolt. All of my life, I had listened to the communist lies. They had lied about everything – it should have dawned on me that they would lie about God, too. There it was, it was unmistakably true – God *does* exist!

The presence that surrounded me became thicker and more palpable, and I began to shake. I shook so hard that I fell down into the dirt. I shook and cried all day on that mountaintop, merely from the discovery that there really is a God. "Who are You?" I cried out. "What are You? I can't see You, but I can tell that You are there!" I was crying loudly, desperately wanting to know more about this invisible God, whose presence I could somehow feel. I felt an overwhelming need to immediately know everything!

Hours passed as I became lost in the moment. Finally, I became aware that it was getting darker and colder. I knew that I had to leave while there was still a little light to find my way down the mountain. It seemed there was nothing else to do but go to the house of the Jesus people.

My eyes and face were swollen from crying all day – I must have looked a mess. They opened the front door, took one look at me and smiled knowingly, "Ah-h-h Georgian, come on in!"

A Vision

They began playing their guitars and singing loud and energetically — this time I did not care what they played or how bad it sounded, because I could now sense they were connecting with the God I had just discovered. After two months of their witnessing, this Bulgarian was finally "getting it," and my new friends were ecstatic.

As they were shouting praises, I saw my first vision — the hands of Jesus came toward me. I could not see His face, but I could see His hands. I fell right into them and landed face down on the carpet as Jesus wrapped His loving arms around me. His peace and love melted me and filled me. From that moment on, I had an insatiable hunger and thirst for His presence. You see, once you taste these things, you find the thought of never having them again unbearable, because they become your oxygen.

The following day, my friends said, "We are so excited for you, Georgian. Now you should ask the Lord to fill you with the Holy Spirit."

"The Holy Spirit?" I asked. I had no idea what they were talking about.

"Oh yeah, ask God to baptize you in His Spirit and power. Just you wait and see — it is going to be great!"

Jesus wrapped His loving arms around me. His peace and love melted me and filled me. From that moment on I had an insatiable hunger and thirst for His presence. You see, once you taste these things, you find the thought of never having them again unbearable, because they become your oxygen.

I did everything that I could think of to ask for the Holy Spirit, but nothing happened. I really wanted this, and so I returned to my friends to ask them what was wrong, why wasn't it working? They told me, "Nothing is wrong… just keep asking and soon you will feel Him."

I walked away and asked again for the Holy Spirit. I waited but still nothing happened. I came back and questioned my friends again, "Is this Holy Spirit part of God or what?"

"Yes, yes," they told me, "Wait, you'll see. Just ask Him to fill you."

So, I continued asking over and over again for nearly a week, but nothing happened. Finally, I said to my friends, "Be honest and tell me what's wrong? Something has to be wrong with me because I'm asking but I'm not getting anything."

They said, "Chill out, Georgian, there's nothing wrong with you, man. You've been a communist all your life … it's been less than a week, you have to just keep asking and—"

"DON'T TELL ME TO CHILL OUT! I lost my family and career because of those communists and I want everything I've missed out on, and I want it all right now! Is it for me and is it good?"

"Yes," they replied.

"Well then, I want it now!" I said emphatically. "Don't talk to me anymore about this Holy Ghost unless I get it. I need to have it right *now* or I don't want to hear another word about it."

Having been constrained by the communists for most of my life, I had a very intense attitude about getting those things I had missed.

THRONE ROOM EXPERIENCE

"All right, Georgian," they said, "we will pray for you." They pulled me into a room, but even before they started praying I began hearing a sound.

It was getting louder, and it was all around me like surround sound. I heard thousands of cheering voices and they were growing louder. They were louder than a soccer stadium full of yelling fans.

Then I saw a curtain open and when I looked through it, I could actually see Heaven. I was at the edge of the Throne Room, so I started to enter.

There were swarms of angels, swirling and screaming in uncontained ecstasy. I could see their backs wriggling but I could not see their faces. God was on His throne and completely covered by adoring angels. "Wow," I marveled, "they're having a very good time."

Next, I saw lightning and fire come out of God. It hit the angels, who could barely handle all of the pleasure. Their wriggling and fluttering swelled with every jolt they received from God. I had never read the Bible, of course, and no one ever told me about Psalm 16:11 where it says, "In Your presence is fullness of joy; in Your right hand there are pleasures forever."

Awestruck, I continued watching and without warning, one of the lightning flashes from God headed toward me. As it neared my chest, before it struck me, I noticed it was a grapefruit-sized fireball and then it went inside my body.

It is difficult to find words to describe what I experienced. It was as if fire, heat, and pleasure entered me all at once. It was really good but in a way, it was too good. I really liked it but wished God

I saw lightning and fire come out of God. It hit the angels who could barely handle all of the pleasure. Their wriggling and fluttering swelled with every jolt they received from God. I had never read the Bible, nor Psalm 16:11 where it says "In Your presence is fullness of joy; in Your right hand there are pleasures forever."

could tone it down a notch or two. I could not handle that much – yet, before I knew it – a second fireball was coming straight at me.

Now it was getting *very* intense. As this deluge of pleasure passed through me, I began acting just like the angels – wriggling, jumping, and spinning around.

Bob was the person standing and praying behind me. I turned and hugged him hard and said, "Bob, I love you! I love you! I really love you!" I was squeezing him and raving, "I have this love, Bob, can't you tell?"

He said, "Ah, yeah, man, I know you love me."

"Oh no, Bob," I said, "can't you feel it – the fire and the love? I have this amazing new love – it's the love of God. There's this fire everywhere, can't you see it, can't you feel it, Bob?"

It was getting hotter and stronger, so I ran outside to cool off, but it only increased. Then I panicked, because of the intensity of my experience, and asked the Lord to stop. He stopped immediately. Once released from that incredible feeling, I was instantly sorry and asked myself, "Why did I panic like that, it was so good?" In that moment, I learned to never ask the Lord to "stop." Now I know to say, "More, Lord, just strengthen my inner man to handle Your consuming presence."

VACATIONING WITH GOD

After that experience with the Lord, my life would never be the same. After He baptized me in His fiery love, my heart was forever branded with an insatiable hunger for Him. Someone bought me a Bulgarian Bible and I began to devour His Word – I read it from cover to cover. I would spend ten hours a day reading, meditating on every page and talking with God. Each Old Testament story was like watching a movie. It was as if the Lord literally took me back in time to observe every scene unfold.

Immediately, I identified with Abraham, because he travelled to a foreign country, God visited him and they became close friends. I thought, "I am all alone in a foreign country, longing for friendships and now I, too, could become a friend with God." During one of God's visits, Abraham asked God if he could cook Him a meal and to my surprise God responded, "Yes."

I said to God, "Lord, You are so busy and yet You took time to be with Abraham – it had to have taken several hours to get the animal, slaughter it, and then cook it for you."

"Well," He explained to me, "how else do you become friends except by taking time and spending it together?"

Then I asked God if He would eat with me, too? He said, "Sure." Therefore, I made the very best meal I could. I was very excited as I prepared the table and sat down to eat with the Lord. As it turns out, I was not very good at making bread and it was as hard as a rock. So, I had to warn Him, "Watch Your teeth on this bread, God."

It was comical and very childlike, but a precious moment that I will always cherish. I treasured every meeting with the Lord and did the best I could to show Him how much I enjoyed becoming acquainted with Him, and how grateful I was for the invitation to have this amazing relationship.

For an entire year, I took a vacation from life to be with God. Unconcerned about tomorrow or anything that tomorrow would bring, I was completely absorbed in Him and fully satisfied in my newfound Friend. It was like being in my own private monastery in the middle of Ojai, California – it was an interval of Heaven on earth… my honeymoon with God… a time when I could spend every possible moment with Him.

My heart was ravished with love as He began to reveal what He endured to make our friendship possible – how He sweated blood in Gethsemane, was betrayed, endured a humiliating trial, was tortured and beaten, and then suffered the agony of death on a Cross. Yielding to His passionate possession, I was useless for anything but Jesus and His work on earth. Eventually, I joined with a full-time ministry and after several years of service became an ordained minister.

In the early days of my Christian life, I was a songwriter of contemporary Christian children's songs such as "Music Machine" and "Bullfrogs and Butterflies." Eventually, I met Winnie, who is now my wife, and as a young couple we became the leaders of the band, "Silverwind." We did Christian concerts in churches and stadiums throughout North America, Europe, Africa, Australia, and New Zealand.

Jesus Visited My Hotel Room

One day while we were ministering on the road, the Lord appeared to me in my hotel room and began to talk to me about holiness. He explained that the ability to live a holy life was a gift, just as being born again and receiving a new heart was a gift. He told me to read Romans 6:1-11, and those words exploded in my spirit like an atomic bomb:

> What shall we say, then? Shall we go on sinning so that grace may increase? By no means! We are those who have died to sin; how can we live in it any longer? Or don't you know that all of us who were baptized into Christ Jesus were baptized into his death? We were therefore buried with him through baptism into death in order that, just as Christ was raised from the dead through the glory of the Father, we too may live a new life.

> For if we have been united with him in a death like his, we will certainly also be united with him in a resurrection like his. For we know that our old self was crucified with him so that the body ruled by sin might be done away with, that we should no longer be slaves to sin – because anyone who has died has been set free from sin.

> Now if we died with Christ, we believe that we will also live with him. For we know that since Christ was raised from the dead, he cannot die again; death no longer has mastery over him. The death he died, he died to sin once for all; but the life he lives, he lives to God.

> In the same way, count yourselves dead to sin but alive to God in Christ Jesus.

Then the Lord said, "Now, just like it says in verse eleven, go ahead, 'reckon yourself dead to sin' and everything that has to do with satan and his lies – and be alive to me." In my zeal, I quickly replied, "I will, Lord; I will start working on it right away!" He answered, "No! Do it now – consider yourself dead to sin *now*."

"Wow, now?" I replied.

"Yes, receive My beautiful gift, open it up and enjoy it. I earned it by giving My blood and My body. Now take and consume it and let it consume you. All you need to do is nurture this gift in response to My love."

"It is all done?" I asked.

"It is finished!" He replied.

Oh, what a revelation! I immediately went downstairs to share it with Winnie who was having breakfast.

God's Discovery Channel

He is so good to bring us into the wide-open spaces of His grace, and today both Winnie and I continue to remain ecstatic over what God has done for us. In fact, Winnie often says that Christianity is like watching Discovery Channel. When we watch it, we learn amazing new facts about nature and creation. We are awed as we learn things that were always true and always existed – things we did not know. That is what it feels like as we enjoy the endless revelation of the finished work of Jesus on the Cross – comprehending all that Christ did for us through His death, burial, and resurrection.

As we spend time with the Lord every morning, our conversation with Him continues as we travel the globe as missionary evangelists. The compassion of Christ has carried us away to Third World nations where we have fallen in love with the poorest of the poor. He has even brought us to minister to communities of people who live in garbage dumps all over the earth. This has become Winnie's favorite ministry and when she goes to these places, her eyes sparkle and dance with the joy of her Savior. I know the people see in her eyes the same leaking substance that I saw coming from the "Jesus people" in Ojai.

Where He leads, we flow together inseparably. We have seen His love and mercy poured out like a river all over the earth. A daily realization of God's abiding presence within us has been like a huge jet, propelling Winnie and me with superhuman energy. Blind eyes have seen, deaf ears were opened, and lives were forever changed by the Gospel.

No matter what you are doing, the Father's top priority is for you to go to Him for your daily hugs, Fatherly words, and affection. His presence not only restores, it keeps you in His loving embrace. After that first hug from the Lord so many years ago, I can still feel His arms holding me.

His arms are extended to you, and He is saying, "Come, let Me love you and satisfy you. You are Mine – I paid to have you all to Myself." Allow His oil of joy and gladness to pour down upon you!

ENCOUNTERING THE HEAVENLY REALM

PATRICIA KING

CHAPTER EIGHT

Heaven is a very real place. Although you cannot see it with your natural vision, it is indeed very real. It is the address of our Heavenly Father and the location of the throne room, the crystal sea, the river of life, the tree of life, and the rainbow-wrapped throne. Heavenly beings such as the Elders, the great cloud of witnesses, cherubim, seraphim, and other angelic creatures gather around the throne to worship Jesus day and night. The atmosphere of Heaven is love and purity. There is no darkness, no sin, no sickness or disease, no bondage, no poverty, and no negativity in heaven. It is a glorious place filled with joy and pleasure.

Believers in Christ have full access, through the blood of Christ, to this glorious place. Christians sometimes dream of the day they will depart earth and be with the Lord in heaven. However, the truth is, every Christian has an invitation to experience the glories of that realm NOW!

My first encounter in this realm was in January 1994, while I was worshiping at a revival meeting in Florida. Preceding it, I had heard one or two testimonies of individuals who had visions or encounters with heaven but I had never considered the possibility of finding this realm myself. I had never believed for or even longed for such an experience.

That night in January 1994, radically changed my life. During the worship service, the revivalist, Elias Antonas, received insight from the Lord that a wind from heaven was going to blow on one section of the auditorium. To my delight, he pointed to our side of the room. When he finished making this declaration, a literal, physical wind, actually blew through our section. The power of the Spirit was in the wind and many of us fell under the power of the Spirit. Maybe I should say, "Crashed under its power." Chairs toppled as row after row of people fell to the floor, few were left standing.

Blasted by this move of the Spirit, I laid on the floor and felt the "weight" of the Holy Spirit in a way that I had never before experienced. Then the revivalist declared, "If any are desiring another touch of the Spirit, make your way to the front. I was so dazed that I did not know if I could make it to the front, but I managed to pick myself up off the floor and staggered to the altar area with others who stood, eagerly waiting a second touch. Before he spoke another word, I fell down again under the power of the Spirit. This time I began to laugh loudly and uncontrollably!

I was embarrassed by my exuberant laughter in the midst of this public meeting, because there was nothing funny said that

Believers in Christ have full access, through the blood of Christ, to Heaven. Christians sometimes dream of the day they will depart earth and be with the Lord in heaven. However, the truth is, every Christian has an invitation to experience the glories of that realm NOW!

could account for this kind of response. The more I attempted to arrest my laughter, the harder I laughed. My mind and my heart were fully engaged in a contest to control my voice. My mind argued with the suitability of such behavior while my heart was overjoyed by what I was encountering. It was all very perplexing to me and the more I questioned the Lord about why I was laughing, the more I roared. After what seemed like many minutes of rolling on the floor with explosive outbursts of laughter, I was conveyed to heaven through a sovereign act of God. In heaven, I had various experiences and revelations.

I Heard All of Heaven Laughing

I heard all of heaven laughing. That is right! There seemed to be a massive crowd of unseen beings laughing hilariously. All of heaven seemed to be laughing in unison. It was as though someone had shared a very funny joke and the whole room (or in this case all of heaven) laughed. I became aware of the presence of the Lord's pleasure and the fullness of joy that saturated the atmosphere of this realm.

I was also aware that there were no concerns, anxieties, or worries in heaven – absolutely none! The "cares of the world" were not to be found in heaven. Then I realized that we are not to worry either; God has everything under control. Everyone in heaven was already rejoicing in His finished work of victory. All in heaven were savoring the full glorious victory of Christ. Then I noticed a curious thing: every time heaven laughed, I would also laugh and when heaven stopped, I stopped, too. I realized that I was divinely connected to the activities of heaven even though I was unaware of it. After Jacob dreamt of the ladder that reached to heaven with angels ascending and descending and awoke with amazement, he declared, "… Surely the LORD is in this place; and I knew it not" Genesis 28:16 KJV). Jacob, had been made aware of the "God-Realm," a place previously unknown to him.

Like Jacob, my encounter in this realm opened up an abundance of new understanding. It was as though *knowledge* that I had not previously comprehended became infused in my *understanding*. While there, I experienced visions within that vision. I saw angels on assignment in the earth and gained wisdom, insight, and revelation of things that were on God's agenda for the coming season. In addition, He gave me an understanding of the laughter by reminding me, "He who sits in the heavens laughs … in contempt of His enemies" (see Psalm 2:4).

Undone and completely overwhelmed by this encounter in the heavenly realm, I was opened up to God in new ways and prepared for other insights and further encounters that would follow.

EVERY BELIEVER CAN EXPERIENCE THE HEAVENLY REALM

In December of 2002, I experienced a 30-day visitation of the Holy Spirit. During that extraordinary interval, He taught me about the access every believer has to the heavenly realm and during that month, the GLORY SCHOOL was birthed. In the Glory School DVD and CD teaching, I build from Scripture, "line-up-on-line," the foundational truth of every believer's access into that realm. You do not need to wait for a sovereign visitation of God – you can access the heavenly dimension by faith. In fact, the Scriptures invite you and in some cases even exhort you to do so! Most who attend the Glory School step into Spirit-led encounters in the heavenly realm after this training. [1]

You do not need to wait for a sovereign visitation of God – you can access the heavenly dimension by faith. In fact, the Scriptures invite you and in some cases even exhort you to do so!

Unfortunately, this is not something that can be conveyed in a few paragraphs, a chapter, or even an entire book. To get it from your head into your heart requires a Holy Spirit guided immersion in Truth. It took me 30 days to really get it. However, I do want to introduce you to Scriptures that will build your faith in this regard.

When I began following the Holy Spirit into heavenly encounters, I fell in love with Jesus and His Kingdom in even greater ways. Remember, we are *in* the world, but not *of* it. Our citizenship and our allegiance is a heavenly one that will last for all eternity. The world and its systems will be shaken, but we are natives of a Kingdom that can *never* be shaken.

Many believers are waiting to finish their days here on earth to enjoy eternal bliss in heaven. Even though a wonderful life beyond our time on earth should be our expectation, the Lord wants you to enjoy that realm now:

Therefore if you have been raised up with Christ, *keep seeking the things above, where Christ is, seated* at the right

---

[1] You can experience the Glory School in your home by getting the CD or DVDs available in the store at XPmedia.com. More information on page 229.

hand of God. *Set your mind on the things above,* not on the things that are on the earth. For you have died and *your life is hidden with Christ in God* (Colossians 3:1-3).

But God being rich in mercy, because of His great love with which He loved us, even when we were dead in our transgressions, made us alive together with Christ (by grace *you have been saved), and raised us up with Him, and seated us with Him in the heavenly places* in Christ Jesus (Ephesians 2:4-6).

For Christ did not enter a holy place made with hands, a mere copy of the true one, but into heaven itself, now to appear in the presence of God for us ... Therefore, brethren, since *we have confidence to enter the holy place* by the blood of Jesus, by a new and living way which He inaugurated for us through the veil, that is, His flesh, and since we have a great priest over the house of God, *let us draw near with a sincere heart in full assurance of faith* (Hebrews 9:24; 10:19-22).

Who may ascend into the hill of the Lord? And who may stand in His holy place? He who has clean hands and a pure heart, who has not lifted up his soul to falsehood and has not sworn deceitfully (Psalm 24:3,4).

After these things I looked, and behold, a door standing open in heaven, and the first voice which I heard, like the sound of a trumpet speaking with me, said, "*Come up here*" (Revelation 4:1).

Blessed be the God and Father of our Lord Jesus Christ, who has *blessed us with every spiritual blessing in the heavenly places* in Christ (Ephesians 1:3).

In My Father's house are many dwelling places; if it were not so, I would have told you; for *I go to prepare a place for you ... that where I am, there you may be also* (John 14:1-3).

Bring Heaven Home

Not only do you have access to the heavens through the blood of Christ, but you can live in the heavenly realm while in the earth. Jesus taught us to pray this way:

"Your Kingdom come, Your will be done on earth as it is in heaven" (Matthew 6:10).

Matthew 3:16 tells us that the heavens opened over Jesus when He came up out of the waters of baptism. Jesus lived under that open heaven and it is clear that He was united with the heavenly realm. The heavens are still open over Christ today. He is in *you* and consequently the heavens are opened over you, too. Christ in you is the hope of glory! Glory is the atmosphere of heaven so you can live as He did, bringing heaven to earth.

Everywhere Jesus went, He manifested the Kingdom of Heaven. His life is an example to all believers. He is our model for life and for ministry today. Jesus said, "The works that I do shall you do also and greater works than these shall you do because I go to the Father" (John 14:12).

Like Jesus, each of us is called to do the works of the Kingdom of Heaven in the earth. Believers everywhere are to bring the realms of heavenly glory into the earth. The day we live in is so exciting. The Gospel of the Kingdom is being preached, the sick are being healed, the dead are being raised, the demonized are being set free, lepers are being cleansed, and the lost are being saved.

You may not be called to be a pastor, evangelist, teacher, apostle, or even a prophet but God has something just as important for you to do. He has a means by which you can bring heaven to your corner of the earth – it is your destiny. Moreover, you will know your finest hour when you discover and operate in that place of influence that God has reserved for you to mirror His glory. Yes, it is truly a glorious hour for both the Kingdom of God and for you!

Bring Heaven to earth! Oh, yes!

That is what we are each called to do.

GOD OF THE
BURNING HEART

JULIE MEYER

CHAPTER NINE

When I was asked to write a chapter for this book, I asked the Lord what was on His heart. For days, I sang to Him during times of personal worship and at odd moments throughout the day:

What is on Your heart, Oh God?

What is on Your mind?

What is in Your thoughts, Oh God,

For these days and for these times?

He answered, "I want to start a revival in the hearts of men and women, from the inside out, so that revival can be released in the earth. I am coming to rearrange, refresh, and revive. I am coming to my own first." Then I was reminded of Jesus' words in John 17:24-26:

Father, I want those you gave me to be with me, right where I am, so they can *see my glory*, the splendor you gave me, having loved me long before there ever was a world. Righteous Father, *the world has never known you*, but I have known you, and these disciples know that you sent me on this mission. *I have made your very being known to them* – who you are and what you do – and continue to make it known, *so that your love for me might be in them exactly as I am in them* (MSG emphasis added).

Even though the Scribes and Pharisees of Jesus' day had studied and pored over the books of the Old Testament and believed they understood God, they only knew "about Him." Unbelievable as it may seem, we can be the same way. We can read great books; go to wonderful conferences, yet still only have a mental understanding of spiritual things. Jesus said, "The world has never known You." Jesus is the only One capable of acquainting us with the Father and we come to "know" Him by discerning the splendor and glory of the Son.

We could ask, why did Jesus think it was important for ordinary human beings with all their limitation to know the Father? Jesus understood that this knowing was not only the desire of the Father but also a desire in the heart of every human being, and that He was the key to satisfying that desire. To know Christ in His glory and invite Him into your heart is the path to knowing God but that is only the first step, there is so much more He wants to do within us.

Fascinating Dimensions of God

Our God is a God of desires. He creates His image in us so that we would have a desire and love for Him in the exact *same way* that He has for us. God loves to *fascinate* us with the various dimensions of Himself and His glory. He wants us to be a people enthralled by and in love with Him because He is captivated by and in love with us.

Does your heart resonate with this song?

He is not a boring God,

He is a burning God,

A God who is consumed with desire,

A God who is a consuming fire,

Our hearts and lives have captured the focus of His gaze!

Revelation 4:11 tells us, "You are worthy, O Lord, to receive glory and honor and power; for You created all things, and by Your will they exist and were created" (NKJV). He created all things and we were created to *know* Him – not merely to "know about God" but to be acquainted with Him personally and intimately. God has a dream in His heart when He thinks about you and me. We know from the Word of God that we are continually on His heart and in His mind.

Psalm 139:1-6:

O Lord, *You have searched me and known me.* You know my sitting down and my rising up; *You understand my thought* afar off. You comprehend my path and my lying down, *and are acquainted with all my ways.* For there is not a word on

God has a dream in His heart when He thinks about you and me. We know from the Word of God that we are continually on His heart and in His mind.

my tongue, but behold, O Lord, You know it altogether. You have hedged me behind and before, and laid Your hand upon me. Such knowledge is too wonderful for me; it is high, I cannot attain it (NKJV emphasis added).

Jesus has a burning heart for *us* and He is knocking on the door of our heart. Some people open their heart's door to Him for salvation but He wants more than that. He wants an invitation to *come in*… and He will continue knocking until we do more than open the door a crack.

He wants to enter, make our heart His home, take over, possess, and consume every part of our thoughts, heart, soul, and mind. He wants to breathe on us His breath of life and begin the process of rearranging, renewing, and reviving us.

> Behold, I stand at the door and knock. If anyone hears My voice and opens the door, I will come in to him and dine with him and he with Me (Revelation 3:20 NKJV).

MY DREAM

I was at home in my living room. It was early in the morning, the sun had just come up and its rays were beginning to dance through my windows, when I heard a knock at the front door. However, this was not a simple knock – it was a constant rhythm that repeated again and again. It immediately had my attention. This knock sounded like a heartbeat: ba-boom… ba-boom… ba-boom. The rhythm and constant vibration at my front door was familiar; my soul recognized it as the sound of my Beloved knocking.

The walls of my house began to vibrate with this rhythm, resounding with this knock of the beating heart. My house was an echo chamber and I could hear the continuous ba-boom... ba-boom... ba-boom. It was as if my whole house joined in with the rhythmic knocking. I knew the One at my front door wanted my attention and I had not even opened the door yet. I thought of Song of Solomon 5:4, "My Beloved put His hand by the latch of the door, and my heart yearned for Him" (NKJV).

I got up to make my way to the door – with every step the knocking became louder and louder. Finally, it was like thunder rolling throughout my whole house, pounding at my very being. I thought to myself, "He is not going to stop. He just keeps knocking and knocking, making a constant rumble – like thunder, ba-boom... ba-boom... ba-boom." The closer I got to my front door the more my own heart pounded.

The Knocking Stopped

Just as quickly as it had begun, the knocking stopped and there was a deep silence. The kind of silence that can be so loud it is deafening, and *this silence* seemed louder than the rumbling of the knocking. All I could hear was the beating of my heart. I put my hand on the latch to open it, and it was as if I could see through that part of the door; for I saw His hand on the other side, holding onto the latch just waiting for me to open it. I looked through the glass panes to the left of my door and saw His face. He was peering

I was face-to-face with a most beautiful Man with blazing eyes.
Jesus is the One with eyes that burn like fire, the One who singers describe with words like, "He's beautiful. He is glorious." This is my Beloved. This is my Friend and I love Him.

through the lattice of my window, watching me. When I saw His face, His gaze captured me.

There I stood with my hand on the latch; it was as if I was frozen in time, gazing into His kind but piercing eyes. Eyes like fire –penetrating to the very core of my thoughts, emotions, heart, and soul. Flames seemed to shoot through the lattice windows like arrows, targeting my heart.

I turned the latch, opened the door, and I was face-to-face with a most beautiful Man with blazing eyes. Jesus is the One with eyes that burn like fire, the One who singers describe with words like, "He's beautiful. He is glorious." This is my Beloved. This is my Friend and I love Him.

I stepped onto the porch and just looked at Him. He was taller than me, with wavy brown hair that fell past His shoulders, and He had very kind eyes. He wore a fluorescent white garment that went to His feet. I remember thinking, *"This man Jesus is a High Priest forever and He reveals who He is even by the garments He wears."* His hands were at His side but I could see the marks where the nails had pierced His skin. He was a real person with real skin that I could touch and feel. He noticed me looking at His wrists and held them up for me to get a better view.

I sensed that He was looking past my outward appearance, past my face and skin – He was looking on the inside. It was as if His eyes were seeing my heart and my thoughts, and I could not hide anything from Him. Suddenly, everything that I was thinking seemed to be amplified as if I was shouting them aloud. I looked around thinking, *Who is yelling my thoughts?* When Jesus is at your door, you need not speak with your mouth, for thoughts are the language of the Spirit, and they are loud and precise.

He said, "Many people open the door, but very few actually invite me inside. I want access to all of the hidden and secret places ... I want entrance into every room and every part of your life."

HE DECLINED MY OFFER

I saw Jesus lean into the door and peer into my house. I said, "Would You like to come in?" He replied, "Yes," and stepped into my home. I said, "Come, sit in my living room. It is clean – I just vacuumed and dusted. Or, come sit in my kitchen, it is also clean. Everything is put away and exactly where it should be." Then He said, "No, thank you, I want to go into your closet, your basement, and your attic."

"What?" I cried, "Those rooms are not clean and tidy! There are boxes and clutter everywhere. Let's just stay in here, please! I'll make You some refreshing tea. This part of my house has so much space and it is all clean. You'll be much more comfortable here."

He stood there looking around a moment and then turned His face to mine and said, "Actually, *YOU are the one who* will be much more comfortable if I stay in here." Then He turned and looked out my large picture window as if He was deep in thought. Slowly, He began to speak as if thinking carefully about every word He said:

"Many people open the door, but very few actually invite me inside. The percentage of people who actually give me an invitation to every single room is even lower, yet that is what I want. *That is how it works.* I want access to all of the hidden and secret places. I want to make myself at home in your closets as well as your living room. I want access to your attic, your basement, your office, your kitchen, and your garage. I want entrance into every room and every part of your life."

With that, He turned and walked directly into my bedroom and headed straight to my closet. Immediately, He was everywhere, rearranging, throwing things away, sorting through boxes, even boxes stacked on top of boxes. He was finding things that were so well hidden I had forgotten they were there. He was quick and very thorough. He knew what He was doing. When I thought He must be finished, He continued looking, finding, sorting, and tossing things out. Then He quickly moved to the next room… and the next… and on throughout my house.

In each room, He began the process of rearranging, throwing things away, and finding hidden boxes behind boxes. This time, I noticed something different about Jesus the man, He became one with the Spirit and I could see through Him. I began blinking my eyes, trying to process what was happening. I realized that I was looking at both Jesus the man and the Spirit of God – they are two but One in the same. Then things speeded up when the Spirit of the Lord became like a tornado going through every room touching every space in my house.

It was like watching the Wind of God move through my home, touching and breathing life into everything. Then Jesus looked at me and said:

It's not really about your house; your house is a picture of you. The closet, the attic, the garage, the basement, all the rooms in your home where you would normally never invite people to visit; those are the rooms I am after because they represent the parts of you people cannot see. They are your hurts, your fears, your secrets, your hidden sin, and your brokenness. I want access to those rooms so I can come in, clean, and refresh them. I don't want to just look at the outside, I want to live, dine, and *be alive* on the inside. I want access to your heart, soul, mind, thoughts, and emotions. These are the places where I would come in and dine with you and you with me. This is true fellowship, this is what I am after, and I will not stop pursuing until I have everything.

Be one of the few who actually gives me ownership of every room and space, and I will come in and *set you free*. I will clean the *dust off hidden talents and find the God-given gifts* you've been afraid to use. I will put them in the center of the table *to be used and seen*. I will *live in every room*. I will *bring light to every space*, and I will *breathe a fresh breath* into this house which is a picture only of you.

A Season of Access

With that said, Jesus breathed in and breathed out, and the Spirit of God began to twirl and swirl all around my house, which I knew was a picture of me. Then He said, "If you give me access, I will come in and I will change you so that you are renewed on the inside and shine from the inside out."

He continued, "This next season is all about access. For whoever will give me complete access to every thought, every emotion, every plan, I will come in and take over. I will rearrange, refresh, and revive so that those who know Me are rearranged for My purposes, refreshed for the coming journey, and revived from the inside out."

Suddenly, the dream stopped and began to rewind in slow motion, as if God hit the reverse button and I was watching a movie wind back to the very beginning. I watched as everything that had happened was replayed backward and soon I was at the

Jesus said, "Whoever will give me complete access to every
thought, every emotion, every plan, I will come in and take over.
I will rearrange, refresh, and revive so that those who know Me
are rearranged for My purposes, refreshed for the coming journey,
and revived from the inside out."

very beginning. Although it was a dream, it seemed very real. Now sitting in my living room, I was considering what I had just experienced when I heard a knock at the door. The knock sounded like a beating heart, ba-boom… ba-boom… ba-boom. Again, I could feel the walls of my home vibrating to the sound of the beating heart knocking on my front door.

This time, however, I ran as fast as I could to the door, and my heart was beating even louder than the sound of Jesus knocking. As before, when my hand touched the latch of the door, I looked up and saw my Beloved looking at me through the window pane to the left of our door. I quickly swung wide the door and said, "Jesus, come in. Come in to my closet, come in to my attic, come in to my basement, and come in to my garage. *Jesus, my life is your dwelling place.* Abide in every room and in every space, make it Your own." He smiled broadly and entered. Then… I woke up.

This encounter in the God realm was so real I felt like I had really lived it. It was so real I wondered how it could be just a dream. I even went into my living room, walked to my front door, and looked through the lattice of my window as I had done in the dream. Then I closed my eyes and saw Jesus looking right back at me. So I opened the door and said, "Jesus, come into every room and every space. Take possession of every thought, every beat of my heart, for I am Yours and You are Mine. Let Your dwelling be with me. Live in me from the inside out."

I felt alive… I felt different. I knew that even in this dream God had come to me and shown me hidden things in my life. And in the midst of the dream, God had begun to work on the secret places and rooms of my life. I felt alive… refreshed… and revived!

YOUR ENCOUNTER IN THE GOD REALM

When we cry out for real encounters with God, they truly happen. Christ is actively pursuing us as His bride to make us ready for this season of revival. He is knocking at the door and beckoning His bride to let Him in. Jesus not only wants in the rooms we have made presentable, but He wants everything. He wants *total possession* of every space, every place within our lives. He wants to fill us, heal us, rearrange us, refresh and revive us so that we can go into the world and release a glorious revival. This revival, however, must begin first on the inside.

This was a dream I actually lived, an encounter in the God realm. He loves to come to His own and confront us with the passion of His heart, because *we are the passion of His heart* and *the reflection of Him to the world.* That is why it is so important we let Him in.

We are to be an accurate reflection of God's glory and
His love to a world desperately looking for "something"
they do not know but will recognize when they see it in us.
There is a real life-changing encounter awaiting you in the
God realm.

IT'S YOUR SEASON
FOR ANGELIC
ENCOUNTERS

RANDY DEMAIN

CHAPTER TEN

Angelic interactions with humanity can be found throughout Scripture. From Genesis to Revelation, each time we read that an angel appeared, we are filled with wonder. Angels are messengers and warriors dispatched from the Lord of Hosts to bring forth revelation, provision, and protection.

The scope of their access to heaven and earth is startling. When they manifest to us, they are breathtaking and fearful. Angelic visitations bring the reality of the power and glory of God's unseen realm to our natural senses with light, color, and sound. The purity of their presence is a radiation from the glory realm from which they come. This is most evident when the angel comes straight from the Throne Room of Heaven to speak forth the things of God.

Angels are messengers and warriors dispatched from the Lord of Hosts to bring forth revelation, provision, and protection.

On other occasions, angels have ministered to me in human form, wearing normal attire. This type of manifestation allows them at first to operate on the earth undetected. Once they leave your presence, you may find yourself thinking there was something curious about that person and you wonder about them. You find yourself saying: "Was that… Could it have been…?" Then suddenly, the realization that you were actually entertaining an angel unaware:

> Do not forget to entertain strangers, for by so doing some people have entertained angels without knowing it (Hebrews 13:2 NIV).

A Vietnamese Angel

In 2000, I was involved with a humanitarian aid effort to the people of Vietnam. The entire trip was supernatural. One morning, the group leader asked me to minister to the underground churches in the area. When I asked when and where to meet them, his response shocked and surprised me. He said, "Go out on the front steps of the hotel at 9am and ask the Holy Spirit to lead you to them." This method was necessary to avoid exposing the locations of underground churches to a communist government opposed to Christianity.

As I obeyed his instructions, the Holy Spirit led me to a storefront about five blocks from the hotel. When I looked inside, a woman acknowledged me and said, "Please come in." I didn't catch the fact that she spoke perfect English until later. The Holy Spirit told me, "Go to the counter and tell the woman you are looking for Jesus." Once again, I excitedly followed the leading of the Holy Spirit. The person nodded and then led me to a secret passage in the back of the store. As I entered a back room, I heard a Michael W. Smith song playing for the group of believers who were awaiting my arrival. With the help of the Holy Spirit, I had discovered the local body of Christ and ministered to them. I could not help but wonder if this is how things will be in the last days. How awesome it would be to go about all day being led by the Holy Spirit to people and places only Spirit-filled believers could find!

Later, we traveled to another city and encountered a group of potentially hostile soldiers who had been drinking heavily. We were aware that a life-threatening encounter could ensue, as the communist soldiers may think they have a score to settle with Americans. A few of us watched from outside the hotel, hoping they would soon drink their fill and leave. Our belongings were already in our rooms, so going to another place of lodging was not a convenient option.

As darkness came, the soldiers did not leave but seemed to get a second wind and were becoming very drunk. We prayed to the Lord for help and all of us heard Him say, "Just walk through their midst and go directly to your rooms." We looked at each other, swallowed hard, and stepped into the hotel lobby filled with rowdy drunken soldiers with pistols and rifles. As we walked through them to get to the stairs leading to our rooms, we expected them to take notice, the room to fall silent, and the interrogation to begin. Instead, not a single glance came our way, no eye contact and no disturbance. I remember walking past them, looking directly at them. They seemed oblivious to our presence.

When I reached the foot of the stairs, I looked back at the men following me to ensure they had all made it. That was when I saw a corridor of angels facing each other with their wings spread out. Although they were invisible to normal vision, I seemed to be seeing them through shimmering waves of heat. Then I realized that God had sent His angels to allow us to pass invisibly through the danger. The angels stayed with us through the early hours of the morning until the soldiers finally departed.

When it was time to return to the U.S., a van took us to the airport and dropped us off in an area filled with people who were desperate to find someone willing to provide them a way out of the country. Passing through this pressing crowd, we made it into the terminal. That's when I discovered I had lost my airline boarding pass. I suspected someone outside had taken it from my front pocket, where I remembered placing it. I went to the counter to explain my situation but found no mercy. Even though I had my itinerary and my boarding pass from the flight to Vietnam, the people at the counter said I would have to purchase a new fare, at a cost of $2,500!

I checked my cash – I had about $100. My mind raced through my options: return to the hotel or try to find someone from my very short list of friends in Vietnam who could help me. The group leader suggested that I may have dropped the pass somewhere in

I saw a corridor of angels facing each other with their wings spread out. God had sent His angels to allow us to pass invisibly through the danger. The angels stayed with us through the early hours of the morning until the soldiers finally departed.

the airport lobby; we all searched but to no avail. So we grabbed hands and asked the Lord for help. Then I turned around and began to scan the floor again in desperate hope and faith that we had overlooked it. Suddenly, a Vietnamese man came up to me dressed in nice shoes and perfectly pressed khaki shorts and shirt. The city was very impoverished because of the recent trade embargo, so I knew this man must be someone special.

He asked in perfect English if I had lost my boarding pass. In surprise, I nodded yes. He reached into his shirt pocket and handed me a perfectly crisp boarding pass. I smiled, accepted the pass, and quickly turned to tell my buddies of my good fortune. With a sense of gratitude and relief, I turned back to thank the man, but he had vanished. Then it dawned on me, God had sent an angel to replace my lost boarding pass. God is so awesome!

VOICE OF THE SEVENTH MESSENGER

Since 2004, I have experienced an increase in angelic activity as God continues to protect and provide for me by ministering spirits, and now He has included messengers. The angelic messengers give me understanding of "times and seasons," much as they did for Daniel. They come and speak revelatory insights to give me understanding of things that are and things to come. They always give me scriptural references to verify their messages and to relate to the body of Christ. Many of the messages I have preached since 2004 have come by way of God's messengers, with the Holy Spirit providing confirmation and expanded understanding and instructions. I have found that I need to write and speak of these visitations to achieve a fuller understanding of their meaning.

From 2006 to 2010, angels began to visit me at night as I was going to sleep or waking up. On October 2, 2006, my wife and I had returned to our hotel room and just gone to bed after a great time of ministry and fellowship. I was about to doze off when I heard the tinkling of a bell. I shook myself a little to wake up and looked in the direction of the sound. To my amazement, a human-sized angel in cream-colored attire was standing in the light of the window ringing a small bell. I jumped out of bed half awake and ran toward him. I had told myself a few weeks earlier, "If I ever see another angel, I want to touch it." I quickly decided this was not a good idea, but not soon enough to avoid encountering something like a force field that prevented me from advancing any closer. I immediately understood that touching this angel would not be allowed.

As I came fully to my senses, I stood awestruck as I watched the angel and waited for what was to happen next. Then he looked over at the digital clock on the nightstand, indicating I should do the same. It was 12:22 am. The angel said, "It's 2-2-2 time; listen to the voice of the seventh messenger." As in past times, the Holy Spirit informed me that the voice of the seventh messenger could be found in the letters to the seven churches of Revelation. I quickly turned to Revelation chapter 3 to find the voice of the seventh messenger, which was the voice to the church of Laodicea.

From previous study, I understood that the church of Laodicea represented the church of our time, beginning from about 1900 until the present day. I felt that a close inspection and response to the angel's message was of utmost importance. As I began to read, the Holy Spirit said, "Tell the church they have two things to hear, two things to do, and two doors to walk through."

The letter to Laodicea was not condemning so much as it was an invitation to come out and be separate from the lukewarm churches of the day and to become overcomers as Christ had overcome. As I read verses twenty through twenty-two, I knew I had arrived at an understanding of the "2-2-2 time" mentioned by the angel:

> Behold, I stand at the door and knock; if anyone hears My voice and opens the door, I will come in to him and will dine with him, and he with Me. He who overcomes, I will grant to him to sit down with Me on My throne, as I also overcame and sat down with My Father on His throne. He who has an ear, let him hear what the Spirit says to the churches (Revelation 3:20-22).

The Holy Spirit gave me understanding of the angel's message:

The two things to hear are – Jesus knocking at the door and His voice.

The two things to do are – to open the door and dine with Him, which speaks of becoming intimate with Him.

Accomplishing those two things brings you to the final "2" in the 2-2-2 series. The two doors to walk through are – the exit door from the lukewarm Laodicean church and the entry door of the overcoming church.

We are to overcome as Jesus did so we may sit with Him at His throne; just as He triumphed over the world, the flesh and the devil in order to be seated with His Father on His throne.

VOICE OF THE SEVENTH ANGEL

One week later after miracle services in Santa Maria, California, I again was dropping off to sleep when I heard a persistent clicking sound. I opened my eyes to discover an angel that looked similar to the one in the previous week's encounter. However, this angel was holding a small box sealed with what looked like a light switch of heavy construction. He was repeatedly flicking the switch

The Holy Spirit gave me understanding of the angel's message:

The two things to hear are – Jesus knocking at the door and His voice.

The two things to do are – to open the door and dine with Him, which speaks of becoming intimate with Him.

on and off. When he had my attention, he said, "It's 4-4-4 time. Listen to the voice of the seventh angel." The voice of the seventh angel is recorded in the book of Revelation, chapter 10. As I read the passage, the Holy Spirit gave emphasis to verses 7-11:

> But in the days when the seventh angel is about to sound his trumpet, the mystery of God will be accomplished, just as he announced to his servants the prophets. Then the voice that I had heard from heaven spoke to me once more: "Go, take the scroll that lies open in the hand of the angel who is standing on the sea and on the land." So I went to the angel and asked him to give me the little scroll. He said to me, "Take it and eat it. It will turn your stomach sour, but in your mouth it will be as sweet as honey." I took the little scroll from the angel's hand and ate it. It tasted as sweet as honey in my mouth, but when I had eaten it, my stomach turned sour. Then I was told, "You must prophesy again about many peoples, nations, languages, and kings" (Revelation 10:7-11 NIV).

The Holy Spirit led me to understand that we are coming into the days of the sounding of the trumpet of the seventh angel.

Things that have been delayed will not be delayed much longer. It is time to eat the little book of Revelation and prophesy afresh to many peoples, nations, tongues, and kings. The Last Days' revelation and the final harvest are on the horizon.

When I asked the angel what the 4-4-4 meant, he gave me Psalm 44:4 where the Lord commanded victories for Jacob, who symbolizes God's people.[1]

ANGELIC PORTALS

Africa and Israel are places of incredible angelic activity. Recently, while in Durban, South Africa, an angel of glorious splendor and brilliance appeared in my room just as I was preparing to minister. He had a golden sash across his chest that said, "Holiness unto the Lord," and he said to me, "The trumpets are being formed and the priests are prepared to sound them." Then he remained for a few moments to give me understanding of his declaration from Numbers chapter 10. The implication of this Scripture is that we are in transition, the cloud is moving.

The Angel said: "The followers of God are waiting to hear the sound to assemble, which is a decree to advance. Although this tone is initiated in Heaven, believers have been created to be able to hear and produce it. It heralds the time when the priesthood of believers is activated to overcome the powers of darkness. It is the sound of victory!"

That night as I ministered, a misty glory cloud of God appeared in the service. Everyone was touched in some manner, some were healed, others filled with the Spirit and refreshed, and some received gold and silver dental miracles. However, the thing I shall

---

[1] The full meaning of my 2-2-2 and 4-4-4 angelic encounters are recorded in a message entitled "Doves of the Latter Rain." More information on page 232.

Angels evoke various kinds of human responses. Sometimes their appearance creates joy, other times comfort. However, angels can also make you feel weak and afraid.

never forget is the sound of joy, triumph, and victory that came from our mouths as we worshipped the Lord in spirit and truth! South Africa will be forever changed by that encounter!

The entire nation of Israel seems to be one huge open portal. I believe Jacob's ladder is still in place and angels are ascending and descending from the throne of God. One night in Jerusalem, I awoke to what first appeared to be seven eyes looking at me from across the room. On closer inspection, I could see it was an angel holding a small version of the menorah, the candlestick in the Temple's Holy Place.

Angels evoke various kinds of human responses. Sometimes their appearance creates joy, other times comfort. However, angels can also make you feel weak and afraid.

This encounter was one of those "weak and afraid" types. As I watched, this angel began advancing toward me with an intensity of purpose. At first, I thought he was going to show me the menorah; instead, he drew near and pushed the burning menorah through my flesh into my chest. I was too weak to move and too afraid to speak. To my relief, I was not physically burnt and didn't feel any pain. However, I was glowing inside. I cannot explain how this could happen without causing injury. While I did not fully comprehend what that visitation meant when it happened, now I understand. God is beginning to restore the menorah—the lampstand of God—to the overcomers, those who are freshly called and activated as a priesthood of believers.

The original menorah was an ornate oil lamp that was part of the furnishings of the Inner Court of the Temple (the Holy Place). It initially symbolized the coming of Christ who—because He would be filled with the Holy Spirit—would be a light to the world. Today, it stands for Christians filled with the Holy Spirit walking the earth as Jesus did, accomplishing what He accomplished and, in some ways, even more.

Here Is the Exciting Part: God is restoring the menorah *in us* – His temple, His church. We know from Revelation, chapters one, two, and five, that the menorah represents the seven spirits of God. God intends for the coming saints movement of the priesthood of believers to be the embodiment of the seven spirits of God – to have the Spirit without measure and to minister like Jesus, who was full of the Holy Spirit and power (John 3:34).

GET READY FOR *YOUR* VISITATION

During a radical encounter with the living Lord Jesus, I was assigned an angel named "Breakthrough Revival." Out of this encounter, I was given the assignment from the Lord to re-introduce my generation to His identity and virtue as the "Lord of Hosts." I was to go to all states in the U.S. and its territories that would invite me. At these places, I was to release the message and ministry of the angel, Breakthrough, to overcome resistance to the next move of God. I spent four years traveling from coast to coast; I went to all but six states, releasing the report of this encounter and the revelation of this new season. Now I am taking this message and ministry to other places and nations.

About a year after I had this encounter with the Lord and the angel, Breakthrough – Breakthrough visited the prophet, Bob Jones, with 11 similar angels. Breakthrough told Bob he had come to the U.S. with me and was preparing the way for the next move of God and harvest. He told Bob that when he visited him again, the breakthrough revival would begin.

Recently, while in Wales, Breakthrough manifested his presence while I was ministering at Tab Life Center. It was an incredible night – everyone that was present recognized that things had shifted in the spirit realm. I have recently heard reports of many visitations of Breaker angels to individuals in the U.S. and around the world.

Get ready for *your* visitation!

Lord, I pray for all who read this chapter, as Elisha prayed for his servant in 2 Kings 6:17. I ask that You open their eyes to see the angelic realm. Lord, release upon Your servants visitations and encounters similar to and exceeding those of the early church. In Jesus' name. Amen.

DISCERNING ANGELS
AND DEMONS

MATT SORGER

CHAPTER ELEVEN

The ability to discern in the spirit realm is crucial for individuals and Spirit-led ministries. By accurately perceiving the spiritual atmosphere, you can operate in a higher dimension of power and authority that will transform lives as a result. This chapter will give you keen insight into operating in and cultivating the gift of discerning of spirits enabling you to bring salvation, healing, and deliverance from demonic influences to the many who desperately need it.

Since 2001, when God launched me into a full-time prophetic healing ministry, we have seen thousands healed and delivered by God's power. When I was saved at the age of fourteen, I began praying for the gift of discerning of spirits. I asked God to make the spirit world more real to me than the natural one. When I sought

By accurately perceiving the spiritual atmosphere, you can operate in a higher dimension of power and authority that will transform lives.

the Lord for this gift, He granted my request, and I began to sense the spirit realm as never before.

As a young person, I developed a very acute spiritual sensitivity and could feel the things around me in the invisible realm. At first, I did not understand what to do with this knowledge, but over time God taught me. He trained me in how to properly use it, direct it, and how to become balanced in this gifting. As I grew older, it became one of the most important elements in my healing and deliverance ministry.

Machine Gun Prayers

One important thing I have learned in the healing ministry is that sickness can come from more than one source. Two people with identical symptoms can have very different origins for their sickness. Sometimes sickness is natural and has a *natural* physical root that needs healing. At other times, the source is spiritual and the root is a demonic oppression. The person *naturally* sick needs a healing prayer of faith, but the other needs to have a demonic influence "cast out" of their body. These prayers are very different, and without discernment of spirits it is difficult to know how to pray effectively.

Many Christians pray "machine gun prayers." They shoot at everything their natural mind can think of in prayer and hope they hit the cause so something will happen. Unfortunately, these kinds of prayers often fail to produce results and that hinders our faith.

However, when we pray with power, authority, and *discernment*, we can hit the target and our faith goes even higher.

DETECTING SPIRITS OF INFIRMITY

Let's look at how to perceive the influence of the demonic in those suffering a physical illness. Scripture clearly shows that there are times when a natural infirmity causes sickness and other times when it is the result of demonic oppression. Discerning of spirits will reveal when the root of an infirmity is spiritual rather than natural, as in the case recorded in Luke 13:11-13:

> And behold, there was a woman who had a spirit of in-firmity eighteen years, and was bent over and could in no way raise *herself* up. But when Jesus saw her, He called *her* to *Him* and said to her, "Woman, you are loosed from your infirmity." And He laid *His* hands on her, and imme-diately she was made straight, and glorified God (NKJV).

From this Scripture we can learn two things. A demon of infirmity had bound this woman, afflicted her physical body for eighteen years, and caused her to be bent over. Jesus discerned the presence of a spiritual affliction through the Holy Spirit and took authority over it. In this particular case, He did not confront the demon directly. He merely said, "You are released from your infir-mity." The moment He uttered that command, the demon had to leave her.

After being released from the spirit of infirmity, Jesus laid hands on her and healed her deformed body. We can understand from this account that she still needed physical healing after the spirit left her because she remained bent over. The effects of the demonic oppression on her back and muscles required healing.

First, Jesus ministered deliverance through the discerning of spirits and then ministered divine healing. An effective healing ministry must also be able to operate in deliverance. Jesus did both and at times we will need to do the same.

We also see this principle of deliverance and healing operating together in the account of the boy who suffered from convulsions. In Luke 9:42, Jesus rebuked the unclean spirit, healed the child, and then restored him to his father.

Jesus did three things during His earthly ministry: He preached repentance, healed the sick, and cast out demons (see Mark 6:12-13). We can also operate in all three of these ministries today.

Jesus did three things during His earthly ministry: He preached repentance, healed the sick, and cast out demons (see Mark 6:12-13). We can also operate in all three of these ministries today.

The Spirit of Trauma

A few years ago, when I gave an altar call for those who needed healing at a Spirit-filled Methodist church in Georgia, a 93-year-old man came forward for prayer with his 91-year-old wife. He could not stand well so he sat in a chair at the altar, with his wife seated next to him. When I looked at the man, my spiritual vision opened and I could see what appeared to be a small black ball on the back of his neck and head – it was a demon.

I walked over and put my hand on his neck but instead of screaming, "Come out!" I calmly but with authority commanded, "In the name of Jesus, let him go." God gave me authority over it and instantly the man looked up with wide eyes. He did not understand what had occurred but, with tears streaming down his face, he asked, "What's happening to me? The pain is all gone!" When asked when the pain had started, he explained, "A year ago I fell over a suitcase and hit my head on the ground. Since then, I've had nonstop pain in my head and haven't been able to sleep well for a whole year."

Understanding this man's situation requires knowledge of how the enemy functions. The enemy often operates through a spirit of trauma, not only in the emotional realm but also in the physical. When a person is traumatized, the enemy may try to take advantage of it. When a person experiences a car accident or injury, a spirit of infirmity can attach itself to the point of trauma to extend the period of pain longer than necessary. This demonic attachment can hinder the natural healing process and prolong the sickness.

Spirits also attach themselves to emotional traumas. Some people suffer grief for years after losing a loved one. Grieving is natural, but eventually healing should occur. When a spirit of grief or trauma attaches itself to an emotional wound, the pain is prolonged. When you discern the spirit of trauma, you have authority to cast it away and bring freedom and healing to the afflicted person.

The older gentleman in this story had an accident and a spirit of infirmity took advantage and attached itself to his natural injury. Although this does not always happen, it did in this case and his problem required more than a healing prayer. First, he needed a deliverance prayer, and the moment the demonic oppression was removed he was healed.

Next, I noticed that he had hearing aids, so I said, "Take out those hearing aids." I laid my hands on his ears and took authority over the deafness. Some deafness is due to a natural loss of hearing but other times it is due to an evil spirit. In this case, it was a spirit of deafness. When I took authority over that spirit and commanded it to leave, the man's eyes widened. He said, "I feel something being pulled out of my ears!" Both of his ears popped open instantly as the spirit of deafness was removed. Some people think, "When you get old, you lose your hearing and sight; it just happens." No! You can be healthy and strong until the day God takes you home to be with Jesus.

When I turned to his wife, I noticed that she also had a hearing aid. I said, "Take that hearing aid out." Her ear immediately popped open and she leaned over to her husband and said, "Well honey, I guess we're not going to have to scream at each other anymore. We can actually hear each other now."

Discerning Spirits in Everyday Life

This gift is not just for church services – it is there when you need it in your everyday life. Operating in this gift can mean life or death for someone. When growing up, I had a wonderful family life. We loved our grandparents—my mother's parents—and when they became ill, they moved into our home so my mom and dad could care for them. My parents cared for my grandparents for nine years.

My grandmother was suffering from congestive heart failure. When her lungs filled with fluid, we would take her to the hospital to have the fluid cleared. Finally, the doctor told us, "We're sending her home, we can't do anything more for her; she is going to die." That night, around two in the morning, I was awakened by a commotion in the house. When I went into grandma's room, I found her in bed, dying. The moment I walked into the room, the stench of sulfur hit me. I asked my parents, "Do you smell that odor? It smells like sulfur!" They said, "We don't smell anything." I began praying and discerned that the odor was caused by a spirit of infirmity.

When I looked again at my sweet grandmother, I saw a big demon sitting on her chest, suffocating her. An anointing rose up in me, I commanded, "In the name of Jesus, come out of her!" and the thing came right off. I could see it still standing in the room like a shadow so I said, "Get out of the room!" It walked through the wall into the kitchen. I followed and told it, "Get out of the kitchen!" It walked out of the house onto the front lawn. Then I finally said, "Get off the front lawn and go a million miles away where Jesus sends you!" It was as if a vacuum cleaner came out of heaven and sucked it up – immediately, it was completely gone. Two minutes later, my grandmother was resting comfortably in bed, breathing normally. Her lungs were instantly cleared and she soon fell sound asleep. God prolonged her life and we were able to enjoy more time with her.

When God gives you insight into the spirit world, He also gives you power in that world to change it!

This is not difficult. You simply take authority over what you discern and God does the rest. It is very important to be able to discern demonic influences when they are present, but as Spirit-filled believers, we can discern not only demons but also angels.

When God gives you insight into the spirit world, He also gives you power in that world to change it.

KEEP IT BALANCED

One important thing about discernment is we need to keep it in the right perspective. If you are a worshiper, an intercessor, or sensitive in your spirit, you probably have the gift of discernment and merely need to develop it. You who do not consider yourself to be sensitive by nature can also grow in this gift. People who in general are *sensitive* can easily operate in the gift of discernment, because they are often intuitive in their spirit. Regardless of what your natural inclination is, anyone can learn to operate in discernment by first praying for it and then practicing this spiritual gift as God enables.

Discerning the presence of both angels and demons is important to keeping the gift balanced. If you only see demons, your gift is half developed, at best. It is also important not to become overly focused on the demonic. You do not want to be constantly fighting demons – that level of spiritual warfare can be tiring.

It is important to always keep your focus on Jesus and operate from the realm of His presence. We serve a big God and the devil is small in comparison. Let's keep everything in perspective.

THE BIBLICAL FUNCTIONS OF ANGELS

Angels have many activities in Scripture. God sends them to:

1. Assist those who will inherit salvation (Hebrews 1:14)

2. Help minister cleansing and purging (Isaiah 6:6-7)

3. Assist in the healing ministry (John 5:4)

4. Bring breakthrough and deliverance (Acts 5:19, Psalm 34:7, Acts 12:7)

5. Give guidance and direction (Acts 5:20, Acts 8:26)

It is important to always keep your focus on Jesus and operate from the realm of His presence. We serve a big God and the devil is small in comparison. Let's keep everything in perspective.

6. Administer judgment (Acts 12:23)

7. Bring prophetic direction and assurance in difficult situations (Acts 27:23-24)

8. Give divine protection from evil and danger (Psalm 91:11)

9. Provide physical strength (Luke 22:43, Matthew 4:11)

10. Obey the voice of His Word (Psalm 103:20)

11. Deliver a word or message from God (Matthew 1:20, Luke 1:13, Revelation 1:1)

12. Separate the wicked from the righteous (Matthew 13:49)

13. Gather the elect at the end of the age (Matthew 24:30-32)

14. Rejoice when someone repents of sin (Luke 15:10)

15. Deliver the Law (Acts 7:53, Galatians 3:19, Hebrews 2:2)

16. Worship God (Hebrews 1:6)

17. Be subservient to Jesus (1 Peter 3:22)

Angels also:

• Have individual names (Luke 1:19)

• Have their own language (1 Corinthians 13:1)

• Can manifest in human form (Hebrews 13:2)

• Appear in dreams and visions (Matthew 2:13, Acts 10:3)

- Are described as winds and flames of fire (Hebrews 1:7)

- Will never contradict the gospel of Jesus Christ (Galatians 1:8)

Discerning the Presence and Operation of Angels

As a young pastor, I had a very powerful commissioning encounter from the Lord that launched me into a healing ministry. It happened on a Monday morning when I was in the church office with the bookkeeper and secretary. As we were processing the offering from the previous day, the Spirit of God rose up within me and I felt a strong unction to dance before the Lord in worship. I obeyed the Holy Spirit and began dancing around the room.

Within minutes, a tangible glory cloud came into the room. The presence of God was so heavy I was thrown to the floor, my spirit was caught up in a vision, and I could not move for more than an hour. During that time, God was revealing to me things that would take place during the coming years of my life.

When I was finally able to sit up, I became aware of a strong angelic presence behind me. Then I could sense a second angel to my right. As the angel behind me enfolded me in its wings, I felt waves of God's glory flooding over me.

The Holy Spirit then spoke to me, "I have commissioned these angels to travel with you. They will go everywhere you go to help you do what I have called you to do." God assigned these angels to travel with me and assist me in fulfilling His call upon my life. A few months later, I found myself transitioning from a pastoral ministry into a full-time prophetic, evangelistic ministry that would be accompanied by miracles, signs, and wonders.

While angels are continually around every believer all the time, there are moments when God allows us to discern their presence. Often when ministering in a church service, I can feel their presence around the altar and moving throughout the room. Even when I discern the presence of angels, I always keep the focus on Jesus and the work of the Holy Spirit. I never emphasize what an angel is doing because I believe all the glory should go to Jesus. However, there are times that I share what I am sensing in the spirit realm, all the while lifting Jesus up as the Savior, Healer, and Deliverer.

THE FIERY BURNING ANGEL

I will never forget when God sent a seraphim angel into a meeting I was conducting in England. During the morning service, while worshiping God, I began to feel heat radiating from a point on my left. When I stretched out my hand into the space to my left I found the air was hot. I thought, "There's a pillar of fire standing next to me!" Then God told me that He had sent a seraphim angel into the meeting. I had a different teaching planned for that morning, but God had a better plan and took over the service.

That evening when we came to the church, the temperature was comfortable. But as the meeting progressed, it became so hot the ushers opened all the windows and doors. People began removing every extra layer of clothing they could. That seraphim angel was back in the room and God was pouring out spiritual fire.

When I stood to speak, God struck me mute and I could not talk for two hours. As I stood staring at the congregation, I watched as the fire of God swept through the place. It was like the coal that touched Isaiah's lips in Isaiah 6. As God poured His holy fire over the people, many were cleansed and gloriously set free. The tangible presence of God became so intense that some ran out of the church into the streets crying out, "The fire of God is in the church!" This fiery angel had been sent on assignment from God to release a holy fire and commissioning to His people.

Angels Bring Breakthrough and Deliverance

There was a time during Bible school, when I was going through a hard time. As I sat in the cafeteria, I turned to my friend and said, "I'm sinking down. I don't know if I'm going to be able to break through this." He replied, "Let's pray." So, we grabbed hands and began to pray. Immediately, I noticed a glorious presence on all four sides of me. I felt angels all around, front, back, and on both sides. As they surrounded me, I could physically feel them pressing against my body, and I fell to my knees and worshiped God. Within ten minutes, I had been gloriously filled and refreshed by the Holy Spirit and received a breakthrough and release!

The Lord commissions angels on *your* behalf, too. There will be times that God sends angels to minister to you. If you are sensitive, you will be aware of them. When Jesus was in the garden during His time of testing, the angels ministered to Him (Luke 22:41-43). After His days of fasting and testing in the wilderness, angels came and ministered to Him as well (Matthew 4:11).

It is possible to discern both the presence of angels and demons in their activities and operations. As you become more aware of the spiritual realm, it will make you more effective in ministering to others. Just observing the activity of an angel can give you supernatural insight into what God is doing at a given moment so that you can move with Him. Moreover, discerning the activity of the demonic will help you minister healing and freedom to people by the power of the Holy Spirit.

WAYS TO DISCERN SPIRITUAL ACTIVITY

God gives discernment in various ways. Anyone can learn to grow in this gift by developing his or her spiritual senses. Following are six ways discernment can operate in your life.

1. KNOW IT (John 4:17-19 and John 6:64)

Sometimes discernment is a simple *knowing*. You do not know why or how you know, you did not reason it out, you just *know*. This kind of revelation hits you on your gut level, not in your head. You may *know* an area of oppression in a person's life or you may *know* a sickness present in their bodies. This often happens to me when I begin to minister and start flowing in the Spirit. I might be praying for people at the altar when I *know* the kinds of sicknesses in the room and begin to spontaneously call them out in rapid succession while God is healing that sickness.

2. FEEL IT (2 Corinthians 11:29 and 7:9)

There are times when God allows you to feel what He feels – His joy or even His grief over sin. Other times you may discern things through your body. Sometimes, I receive discernment by feeling a sickness during a healing service. I feel pains in parts of my body and I know that God is healing someone with an affliction in that area of their body. I know when the person is healed because the pain leaves me. The operation of this gift powerfully releases my faith.

3. HEAR IT (John 5:30 and Matthew 10:27)

Discernment can come by hearing a word in your mind. You may hear words like depression, suicide, loneliness, or rejection.

You might also hear the name of a sickness in your mind, like heart condition or diabetes. When you hear words like this, you can ask God to give you more detail and you become pinpoint accurate in discernment.

4. SEE IT (John 1:47-48 and 5:19-20)

You can also discern by seeing. This may happen in several ways and on different levels. God has given us a "sanctified imagination." It is located in the area of the mind where you see images and pictures. The Holy Spirit can inspire this area of the mind and communicate to you through pictures in your imagination. There have been times, although now more rare, when people can literally see Spirit-inspired images while their eyes are open. At these times, your natural surroundings vanish and you are caught up in a vision or trance that goes beyond the realm of your own imagination.

5. DREAM IT (Acts 2:17 and Matthew 2:12)

Sometimes God will give you discernment in a dream. For example, I once had a dream about a person I knew, who was in an angry rage. I awoke from my dream and said to myself, "I've never seen him in a fury. Why am I dreaming about him being angry?" A short time later, I was present when that person went into a fit of rage, as things that had been pushed down and not dealt with came flooding out. Normally, he successfully covered his anger. Why did the Lord give me a dream that exposed his anger? Was it so I could criticize and condemn him? No. It was so I could pray for him and see God move in his life to set him free.

6. SMELL IT (Revelation 8:3-4 and 2 Corinthians 2:14-16)

There are times God will give you discernment through the sense of smell. I have been in meetings where I could smell the Holy Spirit like sweet incense. At other times, I have smelled Him like a burning fire. When I was in Bible school, one of my friends told me that he could smell the stench of sulfur when a certain student sat down in his row for chapel services. We did not know what was happening at the time, but later understood that God was giving him the gift of discernment. Only a few months later, this student was expelled from school for engaging in serious demonic activity and behavior.

God wants you to become more aware of the spirit realm and more active in it so that you can minister more effectively. Therefore, He wants you to perceive that realm through the gift of discernment of spirits. This gift is not a prize for a select few but is for anyone who desires to become empowered by the Holy Spirit to more effectively minister freedom, healing, and wholeness through Jesus Christ.

HEALING IN THE GLORY REALM

KATIE SOUZA

CHAPTER TWELVE

I speak at meetings across America and everywhere I go, I ask how many people are suffering from a physical disorder. On the average, 85 percent or more raise their hands! This indicates that many in the church are sick and in desperate need of healing. Why are so many afflicted, and what can be done about it?

In this season, the Holy Spirit is releasing a powerful revelation about the connection between the human soul and physical health. Third John 1:2 says, "Beloved, I wish above all things that thou mayest prosper and be in health, *even as thy soul prospereth*" (KJV emphasis added). According to this Scripture, we prosper in our health when we are prospering in our soul. How does that work?

What is the Soul?

We are three-part beings: body, soul, and spirit. Our soul is the combination of our mind, will, and emotions. When we are born again, God instantly perfects our spirit. The Bible says that the same *spirit* that lives in Christ also lives in us (see Romans 8:11).

However, regeneration in Christ does not instantly perfect our soul. Rather, our mind, will, and emotions are placed in a "process of being perfected" to bring every aspect of the soul under the Lordship of Jesus Christ.

This is why Romans 8:29 says, "For whom he did foreknow, he also did predestinate to be conformed to the image of his Son, that he might be the firstborn among many brethren" (KJV). We are *being* conformed – a process –into the image of the Son. The origin of the word translated as *conformed* means "to shape." This indicates our souls must go through a process of adjustment to become like Christ.

Regeneration in Christ does not instantly perfect our soul. Rather, our mind, will, and emotions are placed in a "process of being perfected" to bring every aspect of the soul under the Lordship of Jesus Christ.

Consequences of Trauma and Sin

Over our lifetime, each of us has become wounded. According to the Bible, the two main sources of soul wounds are traumatic circumstances and sin.

Painful events can wound the soul – a tragic accident or death of a family member can leave a scar on the inner man. Even doctors recognize that a trauma can eventually cause the body to develop physical diseases.

Job is a great biblical example of a person who experienced traumas that wounded his soul. Raiders took all Job's oxen, donkeys, sheep, and camels (his vocation and finances); a whirlwind killed all his children when their house crashed down on them (his family), and if that was not enough, Job was then afflicted with painful boils from head to foot (his health). Losses associated with his vocation and finances, family, and health wounded Job's soul, and they often do the same to us.

Throughout the book, Job continually spoke about his soul pain due to the trauma he experienced. In Job 3:20 , he said, "Why is light [of life] given to him who is in misery, and life to the bitter in soul" (ESV). Job's pain from his traumas was so excruciating he wanted to die! The word *soul* is mentioned more often in Job than any other book of the Bible. Every person on the planet has suffered at least one traumatic event during his or her lifetime and most of us have had many such experiences. This means trauma has wounded everyone's soul.

SIN SICK SOUL

How does sin wound the soul? When you sin, or someone sins against you, a wound can form in your inner man. If you have been abandoned, molested, robbed, or verbally abused, those sins committed against you can wound your soul. If you sin against yourself through alcohol or drug abuse, adultery, pornography or some other sin, those sins can also form a wound in your soul.

What causes a wound when someone sins against us? First Corinthians 8:12 explains, "Thus, sinning against your brothers and wounding their conscience [soul] when it is weak, you sin against

Christ" (ESV). According to this verse, when someone sins against their brother it can wound their "conscience." The word *conscience* in Greek means "the soul"! Thus, when someone sins against you, it can wound your soul.

Now look at scriptural confirmation that sinning against yourself also wounds you: "The Lord binds up the hurt of His people, and heals their wound [inflicted by Him because of their sins]" (Isaiah 30:26 AMP). Also, Micah 6:13 says, "Therefore I will also make *you* sick by striking you, by making you desolate because of your sins" (NKJV). Once again, the Bible affirms that sinning causes us to be stricken with a wound, a wound that can cause eventual physical sickness.

The Word says that all have sinned and fallen short of the glory of God (see Romans 3:23). Since everyone *has* sinned, all of us *have* wounds in our souls and, unfortunately, those wounds can cause diseases and disorders.

Terrorist of the Soul

Because sin creates wounds, demonic powers have a legal right to torment us. Sin is an open door to the enemy; it gives him the legal right to afflict you, even giving you a physical disease. The soul is the place where the enemy looks for an open door to attack you. "*For the enemy has persecuted my soul*, he has crushed my life to the ground; he has made me to dwell in darkness, like those who have long been dead" (Psalm 143:3 NKJV emphasis added).

According to this verse, the enemy persecutes your soul. When he comes against you, wounds formed by sin give him a legal right to attack. One of the reasons the enemy did not have power over Jesus is because He had no wounds in His soul formed by sin or trauma. When Jesus was on earth, He came as a man with a body, soul, and spirit. Philippians 2:7 says, "But stripped Himself [of all privileges and rightful dignity], so as to assume the guise of a servant (slave), in that He became like men and was born a human being" (AMP).

Jesus temporarily set aside His divinity to come to earth as a fully human being to be a sinless sacrifice for the sins of all mankind. The Bible says that Jesus' spirit was perfect and that we get our perfected spirit from Him. However, we are unlike Jesus in that our souls are not also perfect. The Bible says He had no sin or wounds from trauma in His soul so He possessed no wounds.

Because there was nothing in Jesus that would allow the enemy a legal right to persecute his soul, Jesus said in John 14:30, "The prince (evil genius, ruler) of the world is coming. And he has no claim on Me. [He has nothing in common with Me; there is nothing in Me that belongs to him, and he has no power over Me]" (AMP).

One reason that Jesus had complete dominion over satan was because there was nothing in Jesus' soul that was in common with satan. Thus, when Jesus encountered demonic spirits they could not persecute His soul.

In Luke 4:34, we find an example of a spirit recognizing this truth. Jesus was driving a foul spirit out of a man when the spirit said to Jesus, "Let us alone! What have You to do with us [What have we in common], Jesus of Nazareth? Have You come to destroy us?" (AMP). When this spirit looked at Jesus, he found nothing in Jesus' soul that was in common with him so he had no power over Him. However, Jesus had power over the demon.

Demonic powers are able to torment you when you have something in your soul that is in common with them. When God heals the wounds in your soul, you will have dominion over those spirits as Jesus had authority over Legion. Then you can command them to leave!

The Bible tells of many instances where people who were sick due to wounds in their souls had given a spirit the legal right to afflict them physically. Luke 13:11-13 is a good example:

> And, behold, there was a woman which had a spirit of infirmity eighteen years, and was bowed together, and could in no wise lift up herself. And when Jesus saw her, he called her to him, and said unto her, Woman, thou art loosed from thine infirmity. And he laid his hands on her: and immediately she was made straight, and glorified God (KJV).

This woman had a spirit of infirmity on her that was literally bending her bones. What gave a spirit the legal right to do so? It was a wound in her soul; Scripture says she had a "spirit of infirmity." The word *infirmity* in Greek means "weakness and infirmity of the body and of the soul." The spirit was able to bend her spine because she had a wound in her soul! Jesus loosed her from that spirit when He healed her soul!

DUNAMIS DELIVERS

Acts 10:38 tells us, "God anointed Jesus of Nazareth with the Holy Spirit and power, who went about doing good, and healing all that were oppressed of the devil, for God was with Him" (NKJV).

This Scripture says that the Holy Spirit anointed Jesus with "power" and He used it to heal people under the influence of the

"God anointed Jesus of Nazareth with the Holy Spirit and power, who went about doing good, and healing all that were oppressed of the devil, for God was with Him" (Acts 10:38 NKJV).

devil. The word *power* is the Greek word *dunamis*, which means "the power to perform miracles and be excellent of soul." Many times when Jesus healed physical bodies, He first healed their wounded souls! When Jesus released His anointing of dunamis on people, it caused them to become "excellent of soul." Then they could prosper in their health even as their soul was prospered! (See 3 John 1:2).

Do you remember the healing of the woman with the issue of blood? Scripture says that when she touched the hem of Jesus' garment, He felt *power* or *dunamis* come out of Him. This indicates that Jesus healed her physical affliction when He made her "excellent of soul."

In Luke 6, Jesus used His dunamis anointing to heal people of their physical diseases and deliver them of demons:

And he came down with them, and stood in the plain, and the company of his disciples, and a great multitude of people out of all Judaea and Jerusalem, and from the sea coast of Tyre and Sidon, which came to hear him, and to be healed of their diseases; And they that were vexed with unclean spirits: and they were healed. And the whole multitude sought to touch him: for there went virtue out of him, and healed them all (Luke 6:17-19 KJV).

The people Jesus healed in this account were sick in their bodies because of their souls' wounds. The specific power Jesus used to heal them was *virtue*, which is another word used for *dunamis*. When He released dunamis on them, they became "excellent of soul"! Then they were able to prosper in their health. Some were vexed with unclean spirits. Yet when Jesus released dunamis, they were delivered, their soul wounds were healed, and the spirits of affliction had to go!

Jesus passed this power on to His disciples so that they could do the same. Luke 9:1 says, "Then he called his twelve disciples together, and gave them power [dunamis] and authority over all devils, and to cure diseases" (KJV). Jesus gives His disciples today this same anointing to heal people in their souls so they can be healed in their bodies. We have seen countless physical miracles in our meetings as souls were healed – let me share a few stories.

Miracles Due to Dunamis

Dunamis power can heal people of physical afflictions that come upon them through trauma. At a meeting where my team and I were releasing the dunamis anointing, I got some words of knowledge. I heard the Lord say that He was healing someone of the effects of a car accident. Then I heard the words "right ear ringing" and "bone-on-bone." After I released the words of knowledge, a woman came up who had been in a severe automobile accident that caused her to lose the cartilage in her neck and suffer extreme

Many times when Jesus healed physical bodies, He first healed their wounded souls. When Jesus released His anointing of dunamis on people, it caused them to become "excellent of soul." Then they could prosper in their health even as their soul was prospered!

pain from her bone-on-bone condition. When she moved her head, she could hear a grinding. This condition also caused her right ear to ring, and she experienced shooting pain from her ear down the side of her neck.

When she heard the words of knowledge, the ringing stopped, the pain stopped, and she could no longer hear the grinding. God grew back the missing cartilage! This happened when we released dunamis for wounded souls. When God healed her soul of trauma, she experienced a creative miracle in her physical body!

When we released dunamis power at another meeting, I heard this word, "Someone here has an infected cyst. It will pop and drain right now." I spoke the word out and then a few minutes later a pregnant woman came stumbling forward sobbing. A previous pregnancy had ended with a cesarean section and the procedure had traumatized her so much she developed a large cyst in the incision that had never healed. In fact, it got worse and soon afterward she became pregnant again. At the time of the meeting, she had been pregnant for eight months and had suffered this severe infection the entire time. When I uttered the word of knowledge, the cyst immediately popped open and all the infection drained out!

LONG-TERM SOUL WOUNDS HEALED

Now let me mention another characteristic of dunamis. This anointing is able to heal even long-term afflictions. The woman bowed over with the spirit of infirmity had her condition for 18 years because of a wound in her soul. And the woman with the issue of blood was sick for 12 years. John 5:5 tells of the man at the pool of Bethsaida who "had an infirmity thirty-eight years" (NKJV). Again, that word *infirmity* means "weakness and infirmity of the body and of the soul." This indicates that he had been sick all that time due to a wound in his soul. When dunamis power fills a person and they become "excellent of soul," it heals even long-term disorders!

When speaking at a church on the east coast, I taught everyone how to apply dunamis power to their souls to heal their bodies. A week after the conference, a man with multiple sclerosis came into the service; the pastor and several others gathered around him, decreeing that dunamis was filling his soul. When they finished praying and declaring, the man got out of his wheelchair and walked without assistance around the sanctuary! At the end of the service, he was so confident of his healing that he left his wheelchair at the church, walked to his car in the parking lot, got into the driver's seat, and for the first time in 25 years he drove himself and his wife home!

BLADDER INFECTIONS, BROKEN EAR DRUMS, AND BONES HEALED

In New Mexico, everyone in the conference center was focusing on dunamis power when I received an unusual word of knowledge. I heard and repeated, "Someone is being healed of a chronic bladder infection that is related to a history of gambling." A woman in the audience immediately felt a stirring and heat throughout her entire body, especially in her stomach. When she came up to testify about her healing, she told the whole story. She had suffered from a chronic bladder infection for 12 years and had taken countless prescription medication, but the affliction always returned. She also was an avid gambler and said the infections had begun after she started gambling.

At a conference in Arizona, God was healing the hearing of many people, as dunamis power invaded the room. I released a word of knowledge about a left ear being healed. Later a woman testified that in 1975 she was a victim of violent domestic abuse that left her left eardrum broken. Since that time, she was hard of hearing in that ear and had chronic ringing and buzzing. This affliction had tormented her for over 35 years! However, when her soul was healed, her ear instantly opened and all the ringing and buzzing left!

In a meeting in Kansas, when the entire audience was applying dunamis to their souls, I received a word of knowledge that someone with a hunchback was being healed. There was a woman at the event who was bowed over and could not lift herself up. The woman in Kansas could not stand straight, but as soon as she heard that word, she instantly stood up straight as an arrow! That spirit of affliction had to leave when the wounds in her soul were healed by the dunamis anointing!

In North Carolina, I received a word that God was healing a clubfoot. As I spoke it, a woman born with a foot turned in was sitting in her seat, feeling nothing. Fifteen minutes later, however, she got up to go to the restroom, and as she walked up the aisle she noticed her foot was now pointing forward. She was so shocked she began asking people around her if she was walking straight. They all confirmed that her foot was indeed pointing forward! She got the miracle in her bones when her soul became excellent from the dunamis anointing!

A woman at a Georgia conference had painful corns on her feet. She loved to stomp her foot during worship to claim territory for the Lord, but she couldn't because of sharp pain from her corns. As I was releasing dunamis into the meeting, I received a word of knowledge that corns were going to peel off peoples' feet, and immediately the woman's pain left. She told her daughter that the pain was gone and her daughter suggested she take off her boot to look at the corns. When she did, the corns were still there but as she rubbed her foot, they peeled off! She picked the corns up to look at them and found the roots still attached. Her foot had the holes where the roots had been. By the time, she came up to testify the holes had filled in and she was totally healed!

Everyone knows the famous Scripture in Ephesians 3:20, that says God is able to, "do superabundantly, far over and above all that we [dare] ask or think [infinitely beyond our highest prayers, desires, thoughts, hopes, or dreams]" (AMP). That is quite a promise! It happens when the dunamis power of God fills your soul! Let me prove it.

The entire verse of Ephesians 3:20 says:

Now to Him Who, *by (in consequence of) the [action of His] power that is at work within us, is able to [carry out His purpose* and] do superabundantly, far over and above all that we [dare] ask or think (AMP emphasis added).

That word translated "power" is dunamis! Therefore, as dunamis works in you, making you excellent of soul, God carries out His purposes in your life to do "superabundantly above and beyond anything you can imagine!"

NOW IT'S YOUR TURN

You can receive a dunamis empowered miracle, too.

- Set aside time (15 to 30 minutes if possible) to soak in God's presence.

- Make certain you will not be disturbed (lie down or get very comfortable).

- You might find it helpful to listen to soaking or slow worship music.

- Begin to worship God – however, don't ask for anything except for His presence.

- Take as long as necessary to become deep in worship and then ask God to touch and heal your soul. Start by putting the blood of Jesus on any sins the Lord may want to remove. Also spend time forgiving anyone He brings to your mind. Remember that sin makes the wounds so you must deal with that first. Then ask Him to fill your soul with His dunamis power.

- Ask Him to heal the broken places in your heart, to heal traumas caused by distressing events and hurtful things others have done to you, and to heal wounds resulting from your own sins. Do not focus on physical healing but on soul healing. Do not try to encourage Him to deal with any particular soul wound; instead, allow God to do what He wants to do.

- You may experience a vision or memory of a past event God wants to heal, or you may not. He may communicate with you in some way or He may not. Continue soaking in God's presence until you feel His peace saturate you.

- When you must stop, thank the Lord for healing your heart and your body.

- Begin to make soaking in God's dunamis power a part of your devotional time with Him as often as possible and you will see results.

In the Presence of Angels

Joshua Mills

CHAPTER THIRTEEN

In the midst of sounds of worship and beautiful singing, I can still remember the first time I watched angels flying in circles above my head, gliding with ease around the ceiling of the church sanctuary. I was a very young child when I watched angels in this way. They were dressed in what seemed to be white flowing gowns, radiating the most brilliant light as they flew gracefully through the air.

At the time, seeing angels seemed normal because both my friend Sara and I could see them in this vivid way. We would sit together at church, on the right side of the congregation, and just stare in amazement as the angels praised the Lord in this amazing way.

One day, we mentioned our visions to an adult in the church and, instead of being encouraged to see further into the supernatural, we were scolded for lying and "making things up." That was the day I stopped seeing into the spirit realm – the day I stopped seeing God's holy angels.

Meeting My Guardian Angels

It was almost twenty years before this glorious realm was re-opened to me. It happened at Calvary Campground in Ashland, Virginia, through a dream. In that dream, I was lifted into an ethereal sphere above the earth, where I encountered three of my guardian angels.

These angels introduced themselves to me and began explaining their purpose and ministry functions in my life. The first angel told me that he was assigned to release creative miracles, signs, and wonders wherever I ministered. He also operated in bringing unusual gifts and blessings from Heaven into my life.

The second angel told me that he administrated the new songs and the flow of Heaven's sound in my life (literally an angel of praise and worship); the third angel shared that he had been assigned to release holy boldness into my life during times of timidity.

The thing that struck me about all three of these huge angelic beings was their appearance – they looked like me! They were much taller and broader, and each one had a distinct hairstyle and eye color that swirled with heaven's beauty, but still they looked like angelic brothers.

They wore brilliant robes, just as the angels I had seen as a little child. It was through that encounter that I began to realize the importance of the relationship of angels to humanity. I began to research, pursue, and posture myself for further revelations regarding these amazing spiritual beings.

Following that supernatural encounter, I began to sense again the presence of angels in the atmosphere during worship. There have also been times when I could hear them singing along with us as we lifted our voices in adoration to the Lord. I was so thankful that the Holy Spirit allowed me to access this dimension after many years of dormancy in my spiritual walk. The presence of angels has continued to increase in my life and ministry and I want to share some of those times with you so that you can learn to experience them, too.

FIREBALLS OF GLORY

Ever since that realm was re-opened to me, I have had many unusual encounters with angels. They have often appeared in my dreams and many times I've seen hundreds of them gather with us in the sanctuary during times of worship.

Several years ago while ministering in Victoria, British Columbia, Canada; we experienced a great outpouring of God's Spirit and healing power. People were healed of Alzheimer's disease, mental illness, depression, neck, back and joint pain, and red blood cells were recreated in those who needed them. In addition, stomach and digestive problems were cured; lumps and cysts dissolved, and hips, shoulders, and ankles were touched by the healing flow of the Holy Spirit. Deaf ears were opened and sight was restored to the blind!

Many people also received tremendous financial miracles as they sowed generously into the open-heaven atmosphere present in those meetings! During this time of tremendous outpouring, I had another unusual encounter with an angel in my hotel room. This angel spoke to me and then threw a flaming fireball for me to catch! The details of that encounter are on my CD, "Ministering with Angels."

When preaching the following day, this same angel appeared at the back of the sanctuary and proceeded to pull down another fireball from heaven and throw it at me! To catch it, I had to leap from behind the pulpit, race over to the left side of the sanctuary, and reach over the heads of the people seated there! It was wild!

As soon as I caught this fireball, it exploded and discharged a golden dust over my hands, my arms and my face, as well as over those who were sitting beneath this supernatural explosion! This fireball was also filled with words of knowledge! It is impossible to put into words the powerful and tangible weight of the glory of God we experienced that night.

Following is Pastor Susan McLean's first-hand account of those meetings:

"People traveled from Salmon Arm, Prince George and other cities to attend the Days of Glory meetings with Joshua Mills in Victoria, and they were not disappointed. Visible manifestations of God's glory occurred in all meetings with a deluge of golden dust on the last night. An angel met Joshua at the door of his hotel room, the night before, and threw him a fiery ball of glory.

"The last night the same angel appeared in the meeting and threw him fiery balls of glory. The people in the

Angels have often appeared in my dreams and many times I've seen hundreds of them gather with us in the sanctuary during times of worship.

meeting did not see the angel, but many saw and heard Joshua run forward to catch the ball that then exploded in the air. It was awe inspiring to see manifestations of the supernatural come into the natural realm! Joshua went out into the crowd, touching people on their foreheads and praying for them, and everywhere people were plastered with golden dust.

"As we received testimonies, both during and after the week of meetings, we saw that a few moments in the glory can change peoples' lives forever. People were healed from longstanding painful conditions as they walked into the meetings and while worshipping. People who had struggled with bad habits for years, like smoking, suddenly were free. One lady was completely delivered from a lifetime of shame and intimidation from childhood sexual abuse. Another was set free from years of depression and battles with thoughts of suicide. Several people received dramatic financial blessings, too!"

MORE ANGELIC MANIFESTATIONS

Throughout Scripture, we find angels at work in the lives of God's people in many forms and fashions. An angel appeared to Elijah and baked a cake to strengthen him for the journey ahead. This "angel food cake" enabled Elijah to travel for forty days and nights until he reached Mount Horeb:

As he lay and slept under a broom tree, suddenly an angel touched him, and said to him, "Arise and eat." Then he looked, and there by his head was a cake baked on coals, and a jar of water. So he ate and drank, and lay down again. And the angel of the Lord came back the second

As soon as I caught this fireball...

It exploded and discharged a golden dust over my hands, my arms and my face, as well as over those who were sitting beneath this supernatural explosion! This fireball was also filled with words of knowledge!

time, and touched him, and said, "Arise and eat, because the journey is too great for you." So he arose, and ate and drank; and he went in the strength of that food forty days and forty nights as far as Horeb, the mountain of God (1 Kings 19:5-8 NKJV).

Several years ago, the Lord sent my wife, Janet, and me with a ministry team to the North Island of New Zealand. We spent almost a month releasing the glory of God in numerous churches at various locations. This was an exciting adventure because we were experiencing the tangible presence of God in every single meeting! During this ministry trip, the Lord began to disclose the reality of the angelic realm in a different way.

During several meetings when we witnessed the presence of angels, beautiful white feathers fluttered through the air to fall upon those who had gathered with us in the glory realm. One night as I preached about the reality of the unseen realm, we watched in amazement as heavy curtains located behind me began swaying back and forth.

Even though the room had no air vents and all the doors and windows were shut, some were still skeptical about this manifestation. They assumed that people must have been pushing the curtains from behind. The skeptics went behind the curtains and discovered that what they had witnessed was a genuine manifestation of the angelic realm. That night after the meeting, many people were down on hands and knees picking up the hundreds of tiny feathers on the floor. These small tokens of angelic activity were another testimony to the reality of the presence of God's heavenly messengers.

About halfway through that month-long trip, some of the team members began feeling weary in their bodies due to the demanding travel and our tight ministry schedule. One night after a glorious meeting in Manukau, New Zealand, we returned to our hotel room to discover that God had activated the angelic realm to minister healing power to our physical bodies. The Lord sent an angel to bring us golden leaves from the trees of heaven. We were astonished to find the delicate leaves arranged beautifully on the open pages of the Holy Bible. The Spirit of God revealed to one of the awestruck team members that the golden leaves were edible and a source of strength, healing, and supernatural empowerment.

Just as Elijah had eaten cake provided by an angel and been strengthened, we too partook of a heavenly substance, and by eating the miraculous golden leaves we found renewed strength.

Just as Elijah had eaten cake provided by an angel and been strengthened, we too partook of a heavenly substance, and by eating the miraculous golden leaves we found renewed strength.

Through this encounter, we experienced the Lord releasing angels of physical prosperity to bring wholeness to our bodies. The next day, because of our newly found strength we were able to trek to the top of Mount Rangitoto and back. This was so supernatural! We continued ministering for the rest of our schedule with newfound strength, due to the empowerment we received from the Lord. We rejoiced and thanked Jesus Christ, as He had allowed us to encounter His provision in a new way through the remarkable ministry of angels.

MINISTERING ANGELS IN THE HOME

Last year, while at home late one night listening to Scriptures and working at my computer, I looked up to see a line of angels walking into my bedroom. They were unlike any that I had seen before. I could see the outline, like an aura, around their heads, necks and shoulders, but I could not see their faces or their bodies. By spiritual perception, I knew these angels commonly walked through my house, even though I had never seen anything like them before!

A few nights later, I saw these angels again. I was in my television room watching a teaching DVD about the healing power of God. This time the Holy Spirit revealed to me that these were "Watcher Angels." They were assigned to carry out the precious Word of God that was being decreed through the spoken Word! "Bless the Lord, you His angels, Mighty in strength, who perform His word, Obeying the voice of His word!" (Psalm 103:20).

SEVEN WAYS TO DISCOVER THE ANGELS SURROUNDING YOUR LIFE!

I believe that you and every believer *can* become aware of the reality of angels in your life, but it may require some training.

Oftentimes people do not see angelic movement in the invisible realm because they have limited their vision to the natural dimension.

However, the Bible makes it clear that you can begin discovering the involvement of angels in your life through seven scriptural keys:

One – Spiritual Sensing

One of the gifts of the Spirit is the power to operate in the "discerning of spirits" (1 Corinthians 12:10 NKJV). This gift includes, but is not limited to, sensing the spirit realm and its beings. When discerning in this way, you will not be operating in natural "understanding" – it will be through a supernatural "knowing." Discerning of spirits is accomplished through the power of the Holy Spirit, who bears witness with our spirit when something is or is not of God. In the Bible, we see that Peter discerned Cornelius' angelic encounter through this spiritual ability (Acts 10:30-35).

Two – The Word of God

The Scriptures give us revelation about the operation of angelic ministry. According to God's Word, angels are released:

- Through our praise and worship (2 Chronicles 20:22)
- During times of prayer (Daniel 10:10-12)
- When we speak the Word of God (Psalm 103:20)
- Through our Spirit-led offerings and financial giving (Acts 10:4)

We may not *feel* the presence of angels during these times or even sense them in a natural way. However, through faith in the Word of God, we can have a certainty that these activities release the angelic realm into our lives. I have discovered that something changes in my perspective when I am aware of God's involvement and interaction in my life. Through the Word of God, we are guaranteed the deliverance ministry of angels on a continual basis (Psalm 34:7).

Oftentimes people do not see angelic movement in the invisible realm because they have limited their vision to the natural dimension.

THREE – A PROPHETIC WORD

Sometimes the Lord will speak through someone that the angelic realm is manifesting in a specific place or given situation. When we hear the prophetic word, we can begin to participate in what God is doing. By faith, begin thanking the Lord for His revelation, and become open to angelic movement whether or not you see anything in the natural: "Surely the Sovereign Lord does nothing without revealing his plan to his servants the prophets" (Amos 3:7 NIV).

I have found that when I open myself to a prophetic word, it begins opening up to me. In other words, as I have faith to believe, suddenly I begin to see … *first comes believing, then comes seeing!*

At times, I have seen angels as faint outlines or even like moving shadows as I open up to see what the Lord is revealing through the atmosphere in the prophetic realm.

One time while ministering to a small group of believers in a home meeting, I sensed the angelic realm move across the room as a flash of lightning, quickly from one side to the other. This presence came very suddenly, but it opened up the "seeing realm" and I began to prophesy. One lady in the meeting was unsure of the validity of this visitation because she had not felt it in the same way I had. As she sought the Lord and asked Him to reveal the truth to her, tiny feathers began appearing all around her chair. It was quite amazing. The Scriptures declare that when you enter God's secret place, "He will cover you with his feathers, and under his wings you will find refuge" (Psalm 91:4 NIV). The feathers were a sign of God's faithfulness and divine covering.

When we start trusting prophetic words from God, we can begin experiencing the realities they create!

Four – Physical Sensing

First comes believing, then comes seeing!

The more we position our spirit to receive from the Lord, the more we will physically sense the supernatural realm around us. The Bible calls angelic beings "spirit winds" and "servants of fire" (Psalm 104:4). At times you will be able to discern angelic movement as a heat or a tingling sensation; these are the servants of fire in operation. At other times, you may feel a warm or cool breeze as the movement of angel wings creates a flurry of air on your hands or face in worship (Hebrews 1:7).

This phenomenon has occurred to me on several occasions. One time while in the recording studio working on my "Let's Get High" CD, I became so caught up in worship, it seemed as if I was physically in heaven. During this experience, I felt the feathers of angel wings brush across my face with such vibrant and energetic force they felt like the rotating brushes of a car wash.

This experience continued for several minutes as I sang in my heavenly tongues. It was an invigorating and refreshing encounter with the reality of the glory realm. Determining the presence of angelic activity through physical sensing should always be in conjunction with the gift of spiritual discernment.

Five – As a Brilliant Light

Many times the Lord allows us to encounter His angels as brilliant shining lights – you may see an unusual flash of light (perhaps out of the corner of your eye), bright lightning, or multi-colored orbs of light. Many times each color represents a different ministry purpose or function. (Ministry cards are available that explain the biblical and prophetic meaning of various colors. They are useful in discerning the particular ministry function of angels.)

The Bible says that God is the Father of heavenly lights (James 1:17). Because satan can also appear as an "angel of light" (2 Corinthians 11:14), it is imperative to use the gift of spiritual discernment when encountering an angel in this way. God's holy angels always bring glory to Jesus Christ (not themselves), direct you to His eternal Word, and encourage you to obey the Lord.

Six – Appearing in an Open Vision

Angels appeared visibly to the shepherds to announce the birth of Jesus in Luke 2:13-14, to Mary in Luke 1:26-28, and to Joseph in Matthew 1:18-21. Peter was rescued from jail by the visitation of an angel through a vision (Acts 12:6-10), Paul received prophetic revelation by an angel (Acts 27:21-25), and Jesus Christ was strengthened and comforted through an angelic visitation (Matthew 4:11). The Bible cautions us that angels can appear so frequently that we may think they are merely strangers. (This has happened to me on several occasions!) Be careful, you may be entertaining angels unaware (Hebrews 13:2)!

When we start trusting prophetic words from God, we can begin
experiencing the realities they create!

SEVEN – THROUGH A DREAM

Jacob experienced the angels of God ascending and descending on a heavenly stairway through a dream, but this revelation was consummated in the natural world. After this encounter, Jacob exclaimed, "Surely the Lord is in this place and I was not aware of it! ... How awesome is this place!" (Genesis 28:16-17 NIV). We need to be very careful not to disregard the supernatural encounters the Lord enables us to witness through night visions and dreams. Often the Lord uses our dreams to open us up to the realm of the angelic (Matthew 1:20; 2:12-13; 2:19).

HOW TO HAVE ENCOUNTERS IN THE GOD REALM

- Be spiritually alert and attentive at all times, pay attention to the atmosphere around you, and stand in faith, believing for God's promise to manifest the glory realm in your life.

- Regardless of what you sense or see, or do not perceive, angels have been assigned to minister *with you* ... *for you* ... and *all around you* in accordance with God's plan (Hebrews 1:14).

Praise the Lord and thank Him for His goodness. Rejoice,
because He has surrounded you with blessings and
encompassed you about with His holy angels!

DAY OF THE
PROPHETIC WARRIOR

JERAME NELSON

CHAPTER FOURTEEN

The Elijah generation is rising! Elijah's double-portion anointing, along with a new move of God, is coming to the body of Christ. It will be a generation of people, both young and old, who God anoints for this end-time season. They will be a people of radical obedience to the Father's voice, as well as a people who have compassion and love for the lost of the world.

They will prepare the way for the Lord's second coming and be a generation of prophetic warriors who live in the supernatural and reveal the Kingdom of God wherever they go.

EVANGELIST AND PROPHET

What is this double-portion anointing; what will it look like? The anointing of Elijah combines the anointing of the evangelist

The Elijah Generation will be a generation of prophetic warriors
who live in the supernatural and reveal the Kingdom of God
wherever they go.

and prophet. When these two come together, they create a fiery anointing of boldness and power, which causes the hearts of the fathers to turn to the children, and the hearts of the children to their fathers (See Malachi 4:5-6).

You can see this anointing at work in the life and ministry of Elijah. First Kings 18:20-40 tells us of the evangelistic anointing on Elijah. This portion of Scripture shows how God used Elijah to singlehandedly turn the hearts of an entire backslidden generation back to God:

> Then the fire of the Lord fell and consumed the burnt sacrifice, and the wood and the stones and the dust, and it licked up the water that *was* in the trench. Now when all the people saw *it*, they fell on their faces; and they said, "The Lord, He *is* God! The Lord, He *is* God! (1 Kings 18:38-39 NKJV).

When Elijah called down fire from heaven to burn his sacrifice, he proved that the Lord God of Abraham, Isaac, and Israel was far more powerful than the demon-god, Baal. Elijah not only had an evangelistic anointing that called people to turn back to God, but also a strong prophetic anointing. First Kings 18:1-2 tells us that Elijah appeared to King Ahab and declared to him that there would be no rain in the land except by his word. His prophecy came true, as God shut up the heavens for more than three years until Elijah called on God to cause it to rain again. I believe that God is releasing this anointing to the body of Christ right now and raising up a people consumed with the passion of the Lord of Hosts!

They will be a Matthew 11:12 generation, who will truly take the things of the Kingdom of God by force ... walk in the double portion of Elijah, which is also a power anointing ... release true Kingdom authority ... confront the powers of darkness ... and demonstrate the reality of God's love and power to a generation that does not know Him.

THE FINAL PROPHET

Consider the anointing on John the Baptist, the last Old Testament prophet. Luke 1:17 says that John the Baptist came in the spirit and power of Elijah in order to "turn the hearts of the fathers to the children, and the disobedient to the wisdom of the just, to make ready a people prepared for the Lord" (NKJV).

Like Elijah, you can see the anointing of both evangelist and prophet in the life and ministry of John. The Bible clearly says that John lived a lifestyle of calling sinners to repentance. He preached in the wilderness, "Repent, for the kingdom of heaven is at hand!" (Matthew 3: 2 NKJV). He had such a powerful anointing of boldness and fire that many people came to him to repent of their sins and be baptized in the Jordan. This was the evangelistic side of the anointing on John's life.

Now look at John the Baptist's prophetic side. Jesus, Himself, said of John the Baptist that he was a prophet (Luke 7:26). John had one of the most powerful prophetic anointings found in the Bible. He prophesied that Jesus would baptize with the Holy Spirit and fire (Matthew 3:11). In addition, he was used by the Father to call out the Lamb of God and baptize Him in water (John 1:29-

They will be a Matthew 11:12 generation who will truly take the things of the Kingdom of God by force ... walk in the double portion of Elijah, which is also a power anointing ... release true Kingdom authority ... confront the powers of darkness ... and demonstrate the reality of God's love and power to a generation that does not know Him.

34). I believe that God is in the process of restoring this anointing to His church.

Just as John the Baptist was anointed by God with the spirit and power of Elijah to prepared the way for the Lord's *first coming*, we, too, will receive the Elijah anointing to prepare the way for His *second coming*.

Over the last couple of years, the Lord has given me some insight into the spirit and power of Elijah and how He will release this anointing. I want to share some keys the Lord has given me that will equip the body of Christ to allow God's power to move through them in this way. I believe that this anointing is for the *entire body*, not for just a few special people.

Keys to Manifesting the Kingdom of God

First, Obedience Will Reveal the Kingdom

One thing that will mark the double-portion generation is a radical obedience. Elijah was a man of radical obedience. We see this in the power encounter mentioned earlier where Elijah called down fire from heaven and confronted King Ahab and the 450 false prophets of Baal (1 Kings 18:20-40). Immediately before doing that, He prayed, "Lord God of Abraham, Isaac, and Israel, let it be known this day that You are God in Israel and I am Your servant, and that I have done all these things at Your word" (1 Kings 18:36 NKJV).

In this Scripture, we find the key to Elijah's successful confrontation with the false prophets and Ahab – first hearing God's voice, second obeying. This brought the manifestation of God's fire on Mount Carmel. God told Elijah that when he presented himself to Ahab, then He would again release rain on the earth; because of Elijah's obedience, God sent the rain to end the three-year drought! (1 Kings 18:1-46)

Obedience to God's voice causes the Kingdom to manifest. Elijah demonstrated authority and power over the natural elements when he prophesied to King Ahab that there would be no rain except by his word. I believe that God is going to raise up a generation to do the same in our day. He is restoring the true prophetic to His church so that when we speak His word, it comes to pass.

A few months ago, I was in Scotland doing revival meetings in the city of Broxbourn, which is outside of Edinburgh. The final night God, gave me an open vision of a mighty gust of wind blowing throughout Scotland. As I watched this strong gust of wind, I noticed that it was blowing a dark cloud away from the nation into the sea. As the evening ended, I felt the leading of the Holy Ghost to prophesy over the church and the nation.

As I opened my mouth to speak, I found myself saying that God was releasing winds of change in Scotland which would begin blowing a darkness out of the nation that had been hindering the hunger of the church. That He was preparing the way for revival to come again to their nation. Then the Lord instructed me to tell the pastor that He would give a "sign" that this word was from the Lord. After we left, they should expect to see high winds in the natural as a sign of what God was doing in the spiritual. The next day, we went to Mannheim, Germany.

While in Mannheim, I received an email from the pastor of the church in Scotland. He said that about a week after we left Scotland the country had a major windstorm that the newspapers and media dubbed "The Storm of the Century." He went on to say they had winds of over 114 mph, the strongest to hit Scotland in more than a hundred years. Then the pastor mentioned the winds were so strong they had even knocked down his backyard fence. Wow!

God had confirmed His word with a sign in the natural. About a month after that, I received another email from the same pastor praising God for the breakthrough in revival that had begun in his church. Before we came and released the word about the winds of change, there were very few people in his region hungry for revival. He said the citywide meeting they had after we were with them, was their best-attended event in years.

This, I believe, is an example of the operation of the true prophetic in the spirit and power of Elijah that God is releasing in our day. The cause of this manifestation of God's supernatural power was not because of pressing in or doing some sort of prophetic act to get God to move. It was a direct result of simply being obedient to the voice of God, carrying out what He showed me to do.

Jesus walked in obedience in that same way. In John 5:19, Jesus said that He never did a thing unless He knew what His Father was doing. This verse holds a key to displaying the Spirit and power of Elijah. If we can come into a place of seeing and hearing what God wants to do in the earth and then be courageous and do it, we will begin manifesting God's Kingdom everywhere we go.

Following is the true story of a power encounter released by a simple act of obedience. It discloses another side of the evangelistic Elijah anointing and shows how God wanted to make known His love and power to a witch, while we were hanging out in a hot tub.

While on vacation with a friend in Florida, one night my friend and I decided to relax in the hotel's hot tub. As we soaked, the Lord spoke to me about the woman who shared the hot tub with us. He told me she was a "spiritual" woman and that He wanted me to witness to her. In obedience, I started a conversation and asked her if she was "spiritual." She talked at length about her many strange mystical experiences.

Then she asked me what I believed. I told her I was a Christian and believed in Jesus. Immediately, she started laughing and making fun of me. I began telling her how the power of God healed deaf and blind people when I was in India. No matter what I said, she continued mocking Jesus and saying that God has no power.

It was getting late and owner of the hotel came and told us that our time was up in the hot tub. Before we left, the Lord put it on my heart to ask the woman if we could pray for her. She said, "Okay," but she wanted us to know that she was a witch and an avid student of the black arts and the occult. "So what," I told her, "let me pray for you anyway. I'm not afraid of you." She allowed us to pray for her. I took one hand and my friend took the other, but she said, "No, only one of you at a time. I want to be able to center all my energy on only one person." I said, "Whatever," gave her my hand and began to pray.

As I prayed, I immediately had a vision of a rose and began to prophesy. I told the woman that God loved her and, from a heavenly perspective, He saw her as beautiful as a rose even though she did not know Him. I went on to explain the reason He saw her as beautiful is that He created her in beauty in her mother's womb. Then, at that exact moment, the power of God whacked this witch and she began to scream, "You're blocking my powers, you're blocking my powers! No one has ever blocked my powers before!" I answered, "That's because Jesus is the greatest power of all!" The power of God completely overwhelmed this woman.

Then I said to my friend, "Now you pray for her." As he did, I asked God if I could throw a fireball on the woman and the Lord gave me a clear yes. Therefore, I threw a fireball at her by faith, and the power of God hit her and knocked her backward several feet. She started screaming, "What is this energy? I have never felt anything like it before." I told her, "That's the Holy Spirit!" She immediately ran off screaming and we never saw her again.

SECOND, SHARING THE FATHER'S LOVE REVEALS THE KINGDOM

After this experience, the Lord began speaking to me about the power of His love and the double portion of Elijah.

God told me, "Do not focus on the power of your encounter with the witch but on the purpose of it – LOVE." As I had begun prophesying the love of the Father over the witch, God's power overtook her and she had a revelation that God is real and that He is the greatest power in the universe. God went on to tell me that through this encounter, I had tasted the spirit and power of the double-portion anointing of Elijah.

Then He said that He was about to anoint an entire generation with an evangelistic anointing of signs and wonders, along with a true prophetic anointing. Its purpose is to turn the hearts of a generation who do not know Him back to Himself. Signs, wonders, and the prophetic would be a vehicle to convey the message of His love in the last days.

God is raising up a Double-Portion Generation of sons and daughters – those who know who they are in Him and will spread the love of the Father throughout the darkest places on the globe. I believe that God is about to release to this generation some of the greatest prophets and evangelists who will ever tread the earth– those who, out of radical obedience, will walk in mighty signs, wonders, and power.

They will be a people of His presence who carry a heart to restore the lost people of this world to the Father's love.

Will YOU be one of them? You can be!

RUNNING WITH GOD

SAMUEL ROBINSON

CHAPTER FIFTEEN

Have you ever wanted to *run with God*? What would it look like if you gave Him 100% of everything you have? Where would you be? What would you do? Who would you become?

Imagine if we took what we have received from previous generations—the testimonies and impartations of what God did in their lives—and believed that we ourselves could have the same testimonies, and even greater ones!

Jesus said to His disciples:

Most assuredly, I say to you, he who believes in Me, the works that I do he will do also; and greater works than these he will do, because I go to My Father.

(John 14:12 NKJV)

Jesus is telling us through this verse that we would not only do the things that He did, but we could do even "greater things." The possibilities—what we could see and do and where we could go with God—are limitless! I constantly come back to ponder this Scripture.

I love hearing the stories of my dad, Charlie Robinson – how God has used him in powerful ways and he has witnessed the glory of God manifested. I remember when I was around 10 years old, my father had company over and they would talk until late at night about the glory of God. I'd sneak out of my room with my blanket just to hear the God stories, and then I'd fight to stay awake to hear just one more of those amazing reports.

Have you ever listened to testimonies about the awesome things God has done and prayed, "God, could you do that for me, too?" Well, guess what? He can and He will… *if* you let Him.

WHO, ME?

I remember the very first time I had to preach in a church. I was 19 years old and had accompanied my dad on a trip to Indonesia for a conference where he was speaking. Where we were going was very dangerous – at the time there was a lot of conflict between Muslims and Christians. So much so, we had armed guards outside our hotel room because of the very real possibility that we could be attacked during the night.

As my dad ministered at the conference, God moved very powerfully. Many people received healing and several hundred Muslims gave their lives to the Lord. During this amazing conference, a church in another city in Indonesia asked if my dad could speak at their church on Saturday night (which was also the final meeting of the conference).

After the Friday night service, the pastor of the church where the conference was held asked my father if he wanted to speak at the other church Saturday. This would create a problem because my dad was the only speaker at the conference and if he went to the other church, there would be no one to speak at the final service. So, my dad said, "Why don't you let Sammy [me] minister Saturday night at the conference and I will go to the other church." The pastor thought this was a great idea and, with little input from me, they decided that I would minister the last night of the conference.

Having had the privilege of traveling with my dad to many conferences, I knew that Saturday was usually the "blowout" service, and many people would expect healings and impartation. Perhaps I should mention that I had never before preached at a church or anywhere else. The most I had done was speak for ten minutes, and now they wanted me to preach a whole service *and* do ministry time? Huh?

I remember feeling and thinking: I am going to *ruin* the conference. How could God ever use *me* in the way he used my dad? I do not have the testimonies or messages my dad has. Mostly, I had been only supporting my dad in his meetings; consequently, I did not have any messages, let alone the experience or ability to carry off a meeting by myself. So, I did what any 19-year-old in my position would do – panic praying!

WHAT DOES LOVE HAVE TO DO WITH IT?

When Saturday afternoon came, I said goodbye to my dad and quickly went back to the room, where I complained to God about my situation. "How could this happen to me? I'm not ready. I'm going to ruin all the good things that have happened at this conference." In the midst of my lament, a peace came over me and I heard

His still small voice say, "Sammy, I am with you wherever you go. It's going to be alright."

As you know, the Bible says in Matthew 28:19-20, "Go therefore and make disciples of all the nations, baptizing them in the name of the Father and of the Son and of the Holy Spirit, teaching them to observe all things that I have commanded you; and lo, I am with you always, even to the end of the age. Amen" (NKJV).

This statement of Jesus to His disciples was not a farewell speech. He was saying that He was going to *be with them no matter what*. He is with you today, even if you don't feel Him there, He is still right there with you! You are never alone; Jesus is with you wherever you go. You do not have to be afraid, because you have Perfect Love standing beside you. Do you remember what the Bible says about "perfect love"? It casts out all fear!

When I heard the Lord say to me, "I am with you," I knew that everything was going to be okay.

SNOW JOB

I decided to minister on the glory of God, comparing it to the snow on the mountains. That might sound like an intriguing topic to you, but that was not the reason I chose it. I selected it because I had heard my father minister it many times in meetings. However, he had not preached that sermon in this conference, and I knew the message well. So, I thought I would preach it. You know the old saying, "Like father, like son."

You are never alone; Jesus is with you wherever you go. You do not have to be afraid, because you have perfect love standing beside you.

A short time later, the phone rang and the hotel receptionist informed me that the driver for the church was waiting. I remember getting into the car and feeling so much peace. I knew it was my first time ministering, but the peace I felt was as if I had been doing it for many years.

When we got to the conference, the church was packed out! There were well over 2,500 people dancing and worshiping God. I sensed the people were hungry for a touch from Him. The worship lasted for over an hour and the presence of God filled the room.

When the worship ended, they called me up to minister. As I walked up to the stage, it was as if I could feel Jesus walking beside me. He began speaking to me words of knowledge about sickness in people's bodies, and I could feel His love toward those who were afflicted. God healed many people, but it was only the beginning of what He would do that night.

After the ministry time, I started the message and began sharing about the glory of God. I was surprised how easy it was to preach. When the glory of God is with you, you do not have to strive. Then when I got to the part about the glory of God being like snow on the mountain, something incredible happened – *it started to snow in the church!*

Now, I don't mean it was snowing "in the spirit" – snow actually began falling inside the church! When it started to snow, the whole place went wild! Although it was over 90 degrees in the auditorium, snow was falling. Many of the people attending had never before seen snow. Most of them were jumping up and down trying to catch snowflakes while they were falling; the snowstorm continued for 20 minutes.

However, the greatest thing happened when the snow stopped falling. I felt like Jesus told me to have an altar call. This was my first ever altar call, so I simply said, "Come to the front if you want to receive Jesus." While the words were still coming out of my mouth, two hundred Muslims rushed to the front to accept Jesus as their Lord and Savior!

IT REALLY *CAN* HAPPEN TO YOU

The reason I shared this story is to help build your faith that God can use you in the supernatural, too. When we get into situations where there is an opportunity for God to use us, we tend to make excuses to God and list all the reasons why we can't do it. I want to tell you that YOU CAN! God is well able to use you, giving you the same testimonies others have. After all, it isn't about how well you do but what *He* does.

The first thing we have to realize when we want to "run with God" is that we must believe that He wants to run with us – to use us. I know this is a simple truth but when we *really* get the revelation that God wants to use us, it will change the way we think. When we truly believe that God wants to use us, situations that have looked impossible now become opportunities to display the greatness of God.

Second Chronicles 16:9 says, "For the eyes of the Lord run to and fro throughout the whole earth, to show Himself strong on behalf of those whose heart is loyal to Him" (NKJV). He is searching the earth for men and women who will agree with Him and release Heaven on earth everywhere they go. The generation of champions He is raising up will not be afraid to take risks, because the reward is so huge. They are deeply in love with their King, and no risk is too great because of their love for Him. The fear of

> Those who walk in this kind of love will be able to step through any feelings of fear, because they know that God *will* meet them on the other side. Their greatest weapon is the revelation of the love of God, and with this love, they will accomplish amazing things.

making a mistake does not enter their mind, because the Bible says in 1 John 4:18, "There is no fear in love; but perfect love casts out fear, because fear involves torment. But he who fears has not been made perfect in love" (NKJV).

Those who walk in this kind of love will be able to step through any feelings of fear, because they know that God *will* meet them on the other side. Their confidence in God's love is what supports them in the midst of their fear of the unknown. Their greatest weapon is the revelation of the love of God, and with this love, they will accomplish amazing things.

READY FOR ANYTHING?

The other thing that I want you to understand is that we must get into a mindset that *anything* can happen with God. Luke 1:37 says, "For with God nothing will be impossible" (NKJV).

Do you realize what *nothing* means? It means "no thing." I know that may sound strange, but how many times do we limit God by our mindset? We tend to judge Him by our experiences or circumstances instead of what the Word of God says.

Often, I hear people say, "Oh, God won't do that for us," or "He couldn't do that in my life." When we speak words of doubt and unbelief repeatedly, we get what we say. The Bible declares, "For as he thinks in his heart, so is he" (Proverbs 23:7 NKJV).

Many people do not understand that we live in an environment created by our words. Whatever we speak over and over again determines the atmosphere in which we will live. If we constantly speak doubt over our life, we will live in an atmosphere of unbelief, and that will make it impossible for us to see powerful encounters of God's Kingdom invading earth. However, if we live in an atmosphere of faith and belief that *anything* can happen at any time with God, we will witness God doing the impossible in and through us.

"Out of the Blue"

Once when ministering in a church, the Lord told me to believe Him for something that I had never before seen. One of the things that I love about God is He always encourages us to go farther with Him.

While praying before the service, the Lord gave me a "word" about this Joshua generation. He said we are crossing over into our inheritance and would see the prophetic words over our lives come to pass.

While praying into this message, I kept seeing flash images of lightning bolts coming into the church, symbolizing this was a time of visitation. God often speaks to me in pictures and shows me what is going to happen during a meeting. As I was getting these images, I felt that God said I was not only going to see flashes in the spirit, but we would see them in the natural as a sign that He was visiting this church in a new way.

I thought to myself, "We're going to see lightning in the church! What am I going to do?"

Since then, I have learned that when God tells us something that is "far out," we should just believe it. He is not asking us to figure out how it will happen or how to manage it. He merely wants us to believe in Him and His Word. Jesus said in Mark 9:23, "If you can believe, all things are possible to him who believes" (NKJV). What God says to us may sound impossible, but if we will just believe, we'll see it happen in our lives. We shouldn't try to think everything through. Many times when we think too much, we get ourselves out of the place of faith. I always tell people that when God gives us something to do, we need to just do it. Quick obedience to God always brings quicker results.

After I finished ministering that evening, the worship team came up and we began worshiping again. As they were playing, you could feel the atmosphere becoming electric. My dad was with me that evening and I turned to him and said, "The lightning of God is going to show up in the natural in this room. I'm going to take cover." You are probably laughing right now but you would be hiding, too, if you knew what was about to take place.

As the people continued worshiping, the presence of God became stronger and stronger. Then, suddenly, a blue lightning bolt came into the auditorium. Again, this did not happen in the spirit, it actually occurred in the natural and more than 1,000 people saw this phenomenon. You could see and hear the sound of this blue lightning bolt as it came into the meeting, a sign that God was going to visit that church in a mighty way. This encounter from God was so powerful that it cracked the foundation of the church in two places.

A headline in a major national newspaper the next morning read, "Out of the Blue." The article said that a scientist saw a strange, unusual blue lightning bolt hit the city in which we held our meetings. More importantly, from that day on, the church was never the same again. They had three times the number of people saved that year over the preceding year. God is so good!

We must believe God for the impossible. He is always looking for a person who will take Him at His Word, a generation willing to push the limits beyond what they have seen God do before. He does not care how old you are, because He doesn't see the way man sees.

We must believe God for the impossible. God is always looking for a person who will take Him at His Word, a generation willing to push the limits beyond what they have seen God do before.

HEY, DAVID – YES, I MEAN YOU

David is a perfect example for us. When God spoke to Samuel the prophet to anoint a new king over Israel, the Lord led him to the house of Jesse. When Jesse had brought out his sons, Samuel saw the first-born son and thought that this was God's anointed. However, God spoke to him and said, "Do not look at his appearance or at his physical stature, because I have refused him. For the Lord does not see as man sees; for man looks at the outward appearance, but the Lord looks at the heart" (1 Samuel 16:7 NKJV). To find David, Samuel had to look at every son of Jesse and even ask if there were more sons. That tells me that no one is disqualified from being used by God.

You might feel like you are the least of the least, but God sees you as perfect for the job. The only person who can disqualify you from doing what He is calling you to do is *you*! Therefore, stop looking at the reasons you can't do the impossible, and see yourself the way that God sees you. He is for you and not against you. He will believe in you even when you find it hard to believe in yourself. If you will allow yourself to see the way that He sees, you will do the things that He does.

This season, I believe, is the greatest time in history, and we are the very people God has selected to participate in this move of God.

You were born for greatness. The history books can describe you as a person who knew his or her God and did great exploits for Him – or not. God has already made His decision, you're "the man," but you cast the deciding vote. What will it be: *running* with God in the adventure of a lifetime, or *walking*?

AUTHORS AND RESOURCES

PATRICIA KING is a respected minister of the gospel, successful owner of four flourishing businesses, and an inventive entrepreneur. She is an accomplished itinerant speaker, author, television host of "Everlasting Love," and media producer. She has given her life fully to Jesus Christ and to His Kingdom's advancement in the earth. She is the co-founder of XPmedia.com and overseer of Christian Services Association.

THE GLORY SCHOOL – Answer His invitation for more Kingdom experience and divine intimacy! This power-packed, informative school offers you in-depth Bible teaching and training and introduces you into Spirit-led, Kingdom encounters. Discover how to walk more closely with the Holy Spirit, experience the supernatural presence of God, and much more. It is available on CD and DVD sets, as well as mp3, along with a Manual.

Available at: xpmedia.com

STACEY CAMPBELL is a prophetic voice to this generation and has a passion to teach believers to know how to hear the voice of God through proper teaching and strong values. She is the founder and facilitator of the Canadian Prophetic Council. She and her husband Wesley are founders of "Revival Now!" and "Be a Hero." They have ministered in over 45 nations, laboring to see revival and social justice transform the world.

ECSTATIC PROPHECY – In spite of herself, Stacey Campbell began to shake and give prophetic utterance overtaken by the Holy Spirit. The desire to understand this led her on a journey deeper into the heart of God. She explores this remarkable gift in which the Holy Spirit takes over a person's body, soul, and spirit. She offers biblical, historical, and modern-day examples, warns about deception, and explains how to grow in this gifting.

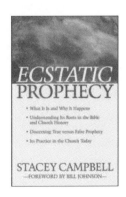

Available at: heroresources.com

FAYTENE GRASSESCHI (Kryskow) is a passionate pursuer of God. She has been in full time ministry since 1997, serving the Lord through church planting, ministry planting, revivalism and social justice activism. She leads The CRY Canada and MY Canada. She is a best selling author, conference speaker and artist. Her messages carry a prophetic edge and are often accompanied by the gifts of the Spirit.

MARKED: A GENERATION OF DREAD CHAMPIONS RISING TO SHIFT NATIONS

God wants you to pray for change in the world, but He also wants you to act. Faytene calls Christians to be history makers in their nations. Sharing from her own involvement with non-profit organizations and speaking to government authorities, she shows you how to be an ambassador in bringing the Kingdom of God on Earth. Join the ranks of a generation of dread champions rising to shift nations for Christ!

Available at her website: Faytene.ca

DR. KAYE BEYER has radical faith and moves in a wonderful gift of healing. She has seen many people healed instantly in her meetings. She believes God for the supernatural no matter what the natural realm looks like. While flowing in a unique prophetic gifting, she also ministers the joy of the Lord to the hurting and those who have lost loved ones. She is president of "We Care for You Ministries."

MIRACLES, MANNA, AND MISSIONS

Miracles, Manna, and Missions will be introduce you to a beautiful child-like model of walking with God into realms of the miraculous. Your hunger for Him will increase, your love and faith will be empowered, and you might even find yourself launched into a powerful missions encounter manifesting the glorious works of Christ.

Available at her website: wcfym.com

DARREN WILSON founded Wanderlust Productions in 2006 when he started his first feature film, **Finger of God**. Later, he created **Furious Love**. Darren taught for 10 years at Judson University before moving into production full time, and he is currently the Artist-in-Residence at Judson. He has a wife, Jenell, and three wonderful children.

FINGER OF GOD

From the streets of Northern California to the mud huts of Africa; from the underground church in China to the Gypsies in Eastern Europe – you will be challenged and encouraged by the extraordinary things God is doing in our world today. Born out of filmmaker Darren Wilson's personal journey of two years, FINGER OF GOD will show you a world of hope and courage. A world where God's fingerprints are found in the unlikeliest of places.

Available at: wanderlustproductions.net

GEORGIAN BANOV and his wife Winnie are a radical power team. Their exuberant childlike praise and deep intimate worship ushers in a breaker anointing for an open heaven atmosphere. The Banovs travel extensively holding apostolic renewal meetings and conferences worldwide. Charged with a heart of compassion for the poorest of the poor, they also host lavish evangelistic feeding crusades throughout the third world.

SONG OF THE ANGELS

Recorded live in the Philippines, Song of the Angels is intimate worship at it's best! This sweet release of spontaneous praise and throne-room adoration also features Georgian on his violin as he plays Heaven's melodies. This album will send your spirit soaring and take you into blissful realms as you worship with the angels before the King of Glory.

Available at his website: globalcelebration.com

MATT SORGER is a prophetic revivalist who travels throughout America and the nations speaking at conferences, prophetic healing revival services and miracle crusades. Matt carries a strong healing and miracle anointing with many instantly healed in his meetings. His ministry is used to help spread the fires of revival and ignite a fresh passion in the hearts of believers to go deeper in their relationship with God. He is also host of the TV program "Power for Life."

POWER FOR LIFE

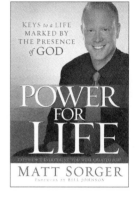

You can live an extraordinary, power-filled life today. Matt's book will teach you how to dwell in real, authentic spiritual power that will transform your entire life and empower you to experience everything you were created for! Overcome your past and be accelerated into the glorious future God has for you.

**Available at: Powerforlifebook.com
and mattsorger.com**

RANDY DeMAIN has been preaching the gospel for over 25 years, and has served as pastor, author, teacher, and church planter. He now travels full time as an Apostolic Revivalist. Randy regularly conducts harvest and healing crusades, training events, and speaks at conferences worldwide. His heart is to see the body of Christ operate, not in word only, but in demonstrations of the Spirit and power.

RELEASING DOVES OF THE LATTER RAIN

Through a series of dramatic angelic encounters and revelatory experiences, Randy De-Main pieces together a series of prophetic clues. These clues are a series of numbers and locations that at first seem unconnected. You will be surprised and delighted as all the clues come together to bring identity to the Doves of the latter rain!

Available at his website: kingdomrevelation.org

(Actual image not available)

JOSHUA MILLS preaches the Word of God and ministers in miracles, signs and wonders. He is a popular speaker, author and recording artist. He has written well over 600 songs. All over North America and around the world, he has been creating a realm of glory wherever he goes, with a message that "praise changes the atmosphere." He and his wife Janet Angela are founders of New Wine International.

POSITIONED FOR PROSPERITY

Understand and develop a lifestyle of generosity... Engage with Angels of Provision... Defeat every spirit of lack and poverty... Learn how to unlock the realms of blessing, favor and increase... Be Positioned for Prosperity!

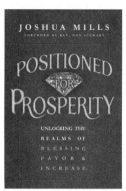

"I know of no one better qualified to help you receive a financial breakthrough in your life than Joshua Mills!" – Don Stewart (Evangelist)

"Excellent Book. Will answer questions... remove confusion and unlock new joy toward life." – Dr. Mike Murdock

Available at: www.joshuamills.com

SAMUEL (SAMMY) ROBINSON is a young man with a passion to see this generation raised up to the fullness of their potential in God. He has travelled extensively, bringing the gospel of Christ to many people groups. Sammy has seen God move in mighty power all around the globe. He moves in a powerful prophetic and healing anointing and has seen many unusual demonstrations of the glory of God in his ministry.

Sammy is part of the team of REVIVAL CANADA, a ministry comprised of a team of prophetic revivalists, teachers and business people, with a mandate to help bring revival to Canada and be-

yond. Through strategic prayer, schools, revival meetings and conferences, their goal is to mobilize and assist in bringing in an endtime harvest of souls.

For more information visit: www.revivalcanadaministries.com

JOAN HUNTER is a compassionate minister, dynamic teacher, accomplished author, and anointed healing evangelist who has devoted her life to carry a message of hope, deliverance, and healing to the nations. Joan's life is one of uncompromising dedication to the Gospel of Jesus Christ, as she exhibits a sincere desire to see the body of Christ live free, happy and whole.

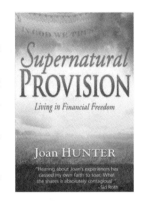

SUPERNATURAL PROVISION – provides believers with the tools to be overcomers financially and live in God's abundance no matter what economic conditions they are experiencing. Don't accept your current difficulties as inevitable and unchanging, look to God anew in faith and He will deliver you and raise you up. Joan will show you how to position yourself to receive that blessing!

"God is going to use this book as part of the transference of wealth to believers." – Sid Roth, "It's Supernatural"

Available at: joanhunter.org

JULIE MEYER is a prophetic singer and songwriter who carries the glory and the presence of God as an abandoned worshipper. Her passion is His presence as she trumpets the message of the Bridegroom preparing His Bride! Julie has recorded several CDs and is the author of two books. Besides being a worship leader at International House of Prayer, Kansas City, she has led worship and spoken worldwide on hearing the voice of God, prophetic singing and worship.

GOD IS ALIVE

Julie's NEW release is a great reflection of what is being released directly out of the International House of Prayer in KC! This beautiful mix of fresh recordings will both draw you into worship and encourage your heart in Jesus. Her popular songs "Unto the Lamb" and "House of Wine" are included on this album. Also featured with Julie on this album is Jaye Thomas and the FMA choir.

Available at: juliemeyer.com

KATIE SOUZA is the founder of Expected End Ministries, a prison ministry touching thousands of lives. She is an international speaker, radio and television host, and author of The Captivity Series: A Key to Your Expected End, which is being taught in facilities across the US and around the world. Katie is a popular conference and seminar speaker who ministers in a powerful teaching and healing anointing wherever she goes.

THE HEALING SCHOOL - 7 CD OR DVD SET

This newly re-mastered and updated series is full of cutting edge, fresh revelation! Learn about demonic kings who cause physical diseases, mental disorders and financial lack. Learn how to become a carrier of the presence of King Jesus, the King over every king! Learn how the light of Jesus can heal your mind, body and soul. Move into the supernatural!

Available at: expectedendministries.com

JERAME NELSON is a prophetic revivalist with a passion to see the Kingdom of God manifested in the earth today. Jerame travels around the US and the nations full time, teaching and preaching on intimacy with God, as well as healing and the prophetic. His heart is to see a generation come into a place of intimacy with God so they are literal manifestations of Jesus in the earth today. He is founder of Living at His Feet Ministries.

BURNING ONES

Burning Ones is a call to action. Christians will be encouraged and motivated to consider seriously stepping in the role of "burning ones" and "dread champions" to spread the Kingdom of God in the earth. Vivid and detailed descriptions of these champions are given throughout the book, supported with biblical examples and modern-day personal experiences, including real-life healings worldwide.

Available at: livingathisfeet.org

Available at the store at XPmedia.com

SIMPLE SUPERNATURAL

Keys to Living in the Glory Realm

Joshua Mills

Every believer in Christ is a supernatural being with a supernatural purpose – called to walk in the supernatural ways of heaven and demonstrate God's supernatural Kingdom here on earth! Joshua Mills shares exciting personal testimonies, biblical keys, and practical guidelines that will launch you into a supernatural lifestyle. Learn how to: Live in the Glory Realm • Win Souls Supernaturally • Manifest God's Word and Heal the Sick and more!

DOMINION SURGES

Prayers, Proclamations and Decrees for Breakthrough in your Life, Cities and Nations

Randy DeMain

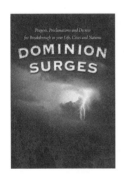

It's time to move forward, overcome and occupy your full inheritance! Dominion Surges will equip you to expand the dominion of the King of Kings in your personal life and where you live. It models how to combine the Word, worship, the prophetic, and prayer into one, unfolding your beliefs into words of action, intent, and pursuit. Get ready to experience breakthrough!

SACRED TIME - SACRED PLACE

A Journal
An Invitation to Spend Time with God

This beautiful imitation leather journal has valuable tools to develop a rich devotional life. It includes practical guidelines to help you have a fruitful devotional time with Jesus, a plan to read the Bible in one year, and plenty of lined pages with a Bible Scripture at the bottom. **Packaged in a gift box.**

CONVERGENCE

Heaven's Destiny Becoming Your Reality

Patricia Bootsma

Paul exhorted believers to 'wage war' for personal prophecies. How does one wage war for a prophetic word and journey from promise to fulfillment? That question burned in Patricia's heart as she sought the Lord about how to walk in the things He promised her through prophecies. Walk beside her on her journey of discovery so the Lord can reveal to you the keys to unlock the doors of your destiny.

GREATER THINGS

41 Days of Miracles

James Thompson and Stephen Court

God's power to perform miracles is beyond limitations imposed by human beings. This book takes you on a miraculous 41-day journey. It begins with stories of present-day miracles followed by passages of Scripture, then brings you to your knees in worship of God, and continues onward with the ministry suggestions that will help you reach out to the unsaved. Believe that even you can be used of God to work a miracle!

SUPERNATURAL MARRIAGE

The Joy of Spirit-Led Intimacy

Dan Wilson, MD

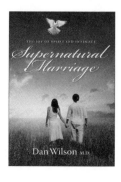

God created marriage for man and woman to reflect that divine union of love, peace, joy, intimacy and fruitfulness. The key to an exciting, fulfilling supernatural marriage is Spirit-led intimacy. Dan Wilson shares his and Linda's journey into supernatural marriage, while sharing important steps to achieving this kind of Spirit-led intimacy - at one as a couple and at one with God.

Additional copies of this book may be purchased through the authors' ministries, bookstores and at the store at XPmedia.com

For wholesale discounts, contact: usaresource@xpmedia.com. For Canadian bulk orders, contact: resource@xpmedia.com.

This book is also available to bookstores through Anchor Distributors.

www.XPpublishing.com

Christian Services Association